PERMIT TO THE PUNJAB

A Celebration of a Lifetime of Friendship with Muslims

ROUTE FOLLOWED AND PLACES VISITED

PLACES VISITED

1. LONDON
2. DOVER
3. OSTEND
4. GENT
5. BRUSSELS
6. AACHEN
7. FRANKFURT
8. MUNICH
9. SALSBURG
10. GRAZ
11. ZAGREB
12. BELGRADE
13. SOFIYA
14. PLODIV
15. EDIRNE
16. ISTANBUL
17. ANKARA
18. SAMSUN
19. TRABZON
20. ERZURUM
21. TABRIZ
22. TEHRAN
23. MASHAD
24. HERAT
25. KANDAHAR
26. KABUL
27. PESHAWAR
28. LAHORE
29. BAMIYAN
30. DIR
31. CHITRAL
32. KARACHI

SWIT – SWITZERLAND
BEL – BELGIUM
NETH – NETHERLANDS
L – LUXEMBOURG
AU – AUSTRIA
Y – YUGOSLAVIA
AL – ALBANIA
GR – GREECE
CZECH – CHECHOSLOVAKIA
BUL – BULGARIA

PERMIT TO THE PUNJAB

A Celebration of a Lifetime of
Friendship with Muslims

HEATHER BOLTON

FOREWORD BY
IAN TALBOT

OXFORD
UNIVERSITY PRESS

OXFORD

UNIVERSITY PRESS

Great Clarendon Street, Oxford OX2 6DP

Oxford University Press is a department of the University of Oxford.
It furthers the University's objective of excellence in research, scholarship,
and education by publishing worldwide in

Oxford New York

Auckland Cape Town Dar es Salaam Hong Kong Karachi
Kuala Lumpur Madrid Melbourne Mexico City Nairobi
New Delhi Shanghai Taipei Toronto

with offices in

Argentina Austria Brazil Chile Czech Republic France Greece
Guatemala Hungary Italy Japan South Korea Poland Portugal
Singapore Switzerland Thailand Turkey Ukraine Vietnam

Oxford is a registered trade mark of Oxford University Press
in the UK and in certain other countries

© Oxford University Press 2006

The moral rights of the author have been asserted

First published 2006

ISBN-13: 978-0-19-547222-6
ISBN-10: 0-19-547222-5

Typeset in Hoefler Text
Printed in Pakistan by
Print Vision, Karachi.
Published by
Ameena Saiyid, Oxford University Press
No. 38, Sector 15, Korangi Industrial Area, PO Box 8214
Karachi-74900, Pakistan.

To my daughter Martha without whose skill and patience I don't think I would have managed with the word processor!

To my son Magnus who gave me encouragement in order to write.

To Eleanor who carefully placed each negative in separate bags, otherwise there would not have been anything like the number of photographs.

To Jo whose legacy enabled me to buy the word processor.

To Bill, who helped me with part of an early draft, and Penny for her friendship, support, revision and suggestions.

To Bilal who gave me fresh heart and help.

Last, but not least Farooq and all his family who gave me the love and inspiration.

Contents

Part One

Part Two

Part Three

Part Four

List of Photographs

Foreword

The opening years of the twenty-first Century have brought 9/11, the sound and fury of the war on terror and most recently the 7/7 London suicide bombings. Amidst media concern with the discredited academic theorising of a clash of civilisations, the spotlight in the West has been on Pakistan and increasingly on the population of Pakistan descent within Britain. There is a worrying mistrust and incomprehension between both the host and the Diaspora community. How should the sentiments in *Permit to the Punjab* be received in such a context? Is this autobiographical account nothing more than nostalgia for a departed world whose innocence can never be recaptured?

This could be one reading. Certainly much has changed both within Pakistan, the Muslim community within Britain and neighbouring Iran and Afghanistan since the author first embarked on her adventure. But even if this was no more than personal nostalgia, the work would be a useful reminder that present mistrusts did not always exist. Nor were they the inevitable outcome of the meeting of the West and the Islamic world.

The book is, in fact, a celebration not just of a bygone era, but of enduring ties and sympathies which cut across cultural and religious boundaries. Their naturalness and ordinariness challenge stereotypes of Islamic fanaticism and of the dangerous Pakistan 'other.' This is not the stuff of headlines. The author's relationship with her Pakistani family may seem remarkable to some western readers, but it is by no means unique—many similar stories could be recounted. Anyone who has ever visited Pakistan will tell of the warmth of the hospitality they receive.

Permit to the Punjab is a more timely work than its author could ever have imagined when she began to put pen to paper. It is in the ordinary human interactions she recounts that hope for a peaceful future rests. While the Bamiyan statues so colourfully described within its pages cannot be restored, the human spirit can still soar above prejudice, intolerance and hatred.

Ian Talbot
Southampton, 2006

Preface

The first journey to Pakistan overland in 1968 was made by Farooq and I in a re-conditioned Morris 1000, and was our adventure or little war. It is a space in our lives which remains fresh. Farooq put it well when he said, 'This was our journey of a lifetime.' Setting off on a trip across Europe and Asia of over six thousand miles in a ten-year old van could barely be deemed prudent. Even though it was at a time when youth was forward-looking, optimistic and adventurous!

The endeavour reminded me of one of my favourite books read at school, *Conrad's Youth*, one of the few to remain with me. I now see the connection between our small venture and Conrad's clipper which set off from Newcastle-upon-Tyne for Bangkok and leaked so much, that by the time it reached the English Channel it nearly had to put to port for good. Needless to say the Clipper never reached Bangkok but burnt out in the Indian Ocean. The moral of the tale, as explained by my teacher was that the impossible had been achieved, even if the goal hadn't! It is better to do your best and fail than set your sights too low.

There is the question of the wider context in time, or the looking with hindsight. Travelling by plane or overland between the two countries was not so commonplace then, nor was there the Internet to keep in touch.

The conservatism which has grown with the maturity of the South Asian community may not now condone a white girl travelling with an Asian. The first journey may not be possible in this day and age. It certainly wouldn't be as pleasurable. The backlash from the Muslim world from western involvement in Iraq has not yet been fully felt.

In Afghanistan today you would see destruction, devastation, and chaos, and hundreds, if not thousands of children maimed from carelessly abandoned land mines—those that have survived the sustained American bombing. The Bamiyan Buddhas no longer exist—they were destroyed by the Taliban.

To prove my escapades took place, the narrative is accompanied by photographs. Some negatives remained dormant over the years, so these are fresh to me.

Some things benefit from a lapse in time, this I believe is one. It has matured and the later journeys added. I always took extensive notes and attempted writing a number of times. After 9/11, because of the negative image painted in the West of the Muslim world, it feels even more vital to express my experience.

Part One

I

From the Khyber back to London

It was still reasonably early in the morning of 4 September when we arrived at Torkham at the foot of the Khyber Pass, at the Pakistani border with Afghanistan. Farooq noted that our mileage from London on the gauge was almost spot on six thousand miles. This was our final boundary crossing prior to our intended destination, Lahore.

It then appeared there was to be a delay. The official was not happy about stamping our passports. In fact, he was very unhappy. He believed we had made the entire journey in order to open a shop! At times he was about to let us through, then tears would well up in his eyes. The subject would change to England almost as if we were old friends. Then once again he would revert to being serious.

'How can you deceive me, opening a shop and you such nice people?' This circuitous conversation made the time slip by into hours. I could not help thinking back over why and how I had arrived here. Only to find we had possibly or very likely, been pipped at the post.

I had met Farooq in 1966, when I was doing a holiday job between Art Colleges, Hammersmith and the R.A. Schools. It was the time, under the Wilson Government, when Employment tax had been dropped or reduced for female employees, and local councils found it cheaper to employ women rather than men. This had resulted in an emergence of female road sweepers in some London Boroughs, and I had become one of them.

Farooq had just opened a stall on the Shepherd's Bush Market, stocked mainly with an array of multi-coloured socks. My flat, situated in a passage linking Lime Grove to the Market, necessitated passing his stall each day from my work at Nottinghill. On returning from a dusty day sweeping, his friendly, open smile had come to my attention. At that time I was mistrustful of good-looking men, he was obviously good-looking, with his mop of thick, black, shiny hair, his round tanned face and column-like neck. My instinct was to avoid such attraction—there must be a catch, or so I thought. But it was not long, conversing only a few

times, that his indisputable charm prevailed and common sense went out
of the window!

As our relationship progressed into weeks then months, it became
apparent that Farooq was unsettled and he had a great yearning to return
to his homeland, Pakistan, albeit just for a visit. Over the eight years he
had lived in London, prior to our meeting, he had made a number of
attempts to do so and for one reason or another, all were unsuccessful.

Personally, I had never had any plans or desire to travel to this part
of the world. Perhaps it was the wonderful, poetic stories Farooq told
me about Shah Jahan, Indian gods and Pakistani folklore that had some
effect and led me to the idea that a trip there together might not be a
bad quest.

Farooq bought me a ten-year old Morris 1000 van and this was to be
our conveyance. Over the following months, the van was parked in a
friend's garden in Acton and Farooq, being a mechanic among other
things, lovingly took the engine apart, cleaned and oiled it bit by bit,
replaced all worn parts and re-assembled it again. At the same time, I
became a dab hand with fibre-glass, filling in holes, dispensing with rust,
generally restoring the van body and finalizing with coats of white paint
and black-painted hub caps.

There were other preparations: inoculations against typhoid and
cholera, a first-aid kit, including salt tablets, spare parts for the van, route
maps from the A.A., a '*carnet-du-passage*' to travel through Iran to ensure
that we did not sell the van there, visas, etc.

Due to our financial limitations, and the Wilson Government's
restriction at that time on money taken out of the country for overseas
travel, it seemed sensible to purchase a Primus stove, water containers
and sleeping bags in order to camp in the back of the van. After reading
A Short Walk in the Hindu Kush by Eric Newby, I had visions of cooking
aubergines as part of our evening meal beside orange Afghan rivers, and
nights of comfort and snug safety in the back of the van.

This, as it turned out, was not to be. The afternoon, the evening and
into the night prior to our scheduled day of departure, a constant dribble
of Farooq's friends and acquaintances arrived from all over London with
packages for us to transport to their respective families back home. There
were dozens of children's T-shirts, jumpers, cardigans, shorts, often many
in the same style but in varied sizes.

It was, in fact, these very parcels which were giving us the problem
now of entry into Pakistan.

The packages had mounted so high that there was no sleeping space left in the back of the van, unless that is, we were prepared to unpack each night and repack each day. Farooq was not the sort of person to disappoint friends and even if I had protested it wouldn't have made the slightest difference. It was only with the greatest difficulty that we managed to fit any of our own things in at all. It also made driving rather awkward as the view from out of the small rear windows was almost obliterated.

A few friends, not those for whom we were transporting items, I have to add, turned out to wish us well and wave us off. My heart felt heavy, I think from apprehension, because I was being torn from something I knew into something unknown, but I was excited, and can still recall that feeling of nervousness and anxious anticipation about what lay ahead.

The sun shone spasmodically in the late morning of 5 August, as we started down the Uxbridge Road toward Dover. There may have been much behind us, including the parcels and months of preparation, as gradually the first feelings of departure were replaced by a feeling of relief. We had actually got things together to start this trip. There we were, speeding out of London in our black and white Morris under the fitful sun.

A smug feeling of acceptance pervaded, nothing could be changed now, anything forgotten would now have to be done without, that is, if we were to catch our booked ferry-crossing, sailing time 18.30. Barely had we escaped the metropolis and we were busily recounting lists of items, clothes, spare-parts, documents, when it appeared that my companion was being evasive, and only after a great deal of prodding and deduction on my part, did I ascertain that he had left his driving licence in Slough! Obviously this was somewhat of a shock. Then there was the annoyance of it all. Not only had I meticulously obtained all the necessary documentation but also that which in extenuating circumstances may have been necessary.

After much talk and argument, Farooq, as only he could, managed to partly convince me that all would be well. I would drive through all borders where documents would be asked for, he would drive between borders, and hopefully whilst he was driving, no one would demand to inspect his license. Although it was with reluctance and a certain unease, I eventually accepted this plan. The show had to go on, it was, after all, a now or never situation, and we opted for now.

2

Ostend to Aachen

Little financial allocation had been made in our budget for hotel accommodation. But we did manage to stack away a little in a reserve emergency fund. On our first night on the Continent, in Ostend, it became necessary to raid the fund. An infection appeared to have located itself in my bladder. Much of my night was spent in a bathtub or on the toilet sipping as much tea as I could lay my hands on to try to relieve the discomfort.

On the second night, not availing ourselves of B&B, we had barely entered Germany and taken a few turnings off the main route to find a remote lane in one of those depressing, rather awesome claustrophobic forests. Farooq had moved to the passenger seat for more leg-room whilst I sat at the driver's side. It was obvious we couldn't unpack all the packages each night.

The dense surrounding forest was fast making it pitch black outside. We were just settling ourselves into our sleeping positions, making the best of a bad job, when we heard an abrupt, sharp tap on the glass at Farooq's side.

This place, I thought, was surely eerie enough without anything like this happening. Something had begun which had a feeling of a nightmare. I could just discern a dark form of a hunched, tall man lurking around the passenger side. Then the repeated rap of knuckle on glass alerted me to higher nervous strains. When I could bring myself to say something, I muttered, 'Ignore him!' Farooq was, in fact, busy winding the window down. I was incredulous, 'Don't talk, Farooq,' I begged, 'Please....' Most of us know the dream when you become panic-stricken and freeze, then wake up with a start, I was at that point emotional but I just couldn't wake up. If I could have done anything I probably would have screamed.

After a little time, it appeared that the two were trying to converse. This man, it transpired, spoke a cross between German and French. Farooq spoke German, and I spoke some French, so they tried drawing me in on questions of linguistics, but 'no cooperation' was definitely my policy. To my mind the situation was preposterous anyway.

'The man says it's dangerous to sleep here.' Farooq managed to ascertain this information and throw it politely my way.

'Where does he suggest we sleep?' I surprised myself at my calmness. Farooq, in his soft husky voice replied: 'He wants us to sleep at his place!'

'No,' I emphatically replied, 'No, We're safer here locked in the van.' Protesting again didn't achieve the desired effect. Farooq remained steadfast.

I speculated on the gruesome stories of murders committed in this awful place that this stranger had fed to Farooq in order to lure us back to his abode.

'He will take us!' Farooq said crisply. I was still convinced that there was something dreadfully wrong with the whole plan. I felt it in my bones. He then told me that we were to give the man a lift in order for him to show us where he lived. I couldn't help asking myself, 'What is this man doing in this dark bloody place, anyway?' But for some reason, although it was on my lips, I couldn't bring this thought to the surface sufficiently enough to speak.

One of the recurring words in their dialogue had been 'six'. This appeared to have some particular significance to the man. At that time it had no significance to me, when there seemed to be more pressing matters at hand. Farooq and I redid the seat swapping exercise again, but neither of us alighted from the van. I was to sit in the middle between the two.

As the stranger sat next to me I scrutinised his profile. Perhaps he had a rather thin nose, was rather straight-lipped, perhaps a rather drawn, pale, hungry look, but nothing very consequential, or so I thought.

Prior to us arriving at his home, he had not successfully conveyed to us that he was a troglodyte. This is not surprising in the circumstances, with our limited communication, and besides at that time, I wasn't fully conversant with the word. It was later I learnt it meant rock-dweller.

The front of his house was part of a rock face, the interior had been carved or dynamited out from the rock behind. There was only one small door visible on the facade, as an entrance, this meant it was possibly the only exit too.

There were no passages inside, and we were led through a series of about five chambers before being introduced to his two children and wife. She was prepared for bed in the couple's bedchamber, so we were quickly led on to a room adjacent to theirs, which incidentally was the last in the series. This was to be our sleeping quarters.

After travelling through the best part of Belgium that day from Ostend via Gent, and Brussels, we were now somewhere close to Aachen, not too far from Maastricht, and tiredness caught up with us both. For my part neither the feeling of foreboding nor the bladder infection stopped me from falling into a deep sleep.

It was only in the early hours of the morning that the nightmare became reality. We were awoken by the man attempting to tear our bed covers from us. My instinct, at last, had been right. Farooq hurriedly leapt to his feet and gave vent to an almighty grunt, more appertaining to that of an animal, rather than human. The sound, I think surprised Farooq himself, it certainly amazed me, and had the desired effect on the man who withdrew swiftly, muttering,

'Six, Six, Six,' pointing to his watch and resembling a mad-hatter. We hurriedly dragged our clothes on, and fled from the scene, retracing our steps through the chambers and out into the relief of morning air.

Now, in retrospect telling this story I see the troglodyte as a kind person who had been genuinely concerned about us sleeping in the forest. From the frugal contents of his home, he wasn't wealthy and his concern with the time was merely because he needed to go to work. Perhaps his home had originally been excavated during the First World War as part of the German Front, and in the Second World War used by the Nazis. Who can imagine what may have taken place there, had it been utilised as living quarters, offices, or even perhaps torture chambers? Or perhaps it always had been used just as an abode.

Setting all that aside, I am now convinced that if the man had not appeared out of the gloom, as he did, perhaps we would have merely remained as bodies in a dank forest! Like the fairytale, two children dead in the woods.

3

Germany to Bulgaria

Other events in Germany, I am glad to say, weren't as uncanny as the previous one. But they did include nearly returning to a town we had passed fifty miles back, which was just averted in the nick of time by doing a U-turn on the motorway access road. Another was when I was driving along a very fast, dangerous three-lane road, the middle lane being common to both oncoming traffic and ourselves. I was overtaking a lorry and we were sucked in so close, that both feared we would end up underneath. I insisted that our van's steering was not as it should be, Farooq insisted it was my driving.

Any confidence he may have had in my driving was now lost, and he decided that he would do it all, apart from, I have to add, through the borders where his driving licence could be requested. The third incident happened on the autobahn, at speed, in driving rain when Farooq's windscreen wiper flew off into oblivion. Although this caused some immediate severe visibility difficulties, it was also to have further repercussions later in our journey.

We were glad the weather improved just as we entered Austria. I remember enjoying the sweeping curvatures of the road, like sailing fast and smoothly down a gradually winding river and bypassing Salzburg. It remained cushioned in the middle distance, nestled there, giving a quick illusive impression of silver spires and white buildings. There had just been a sprinkling of rain, which glistened in the welcome sun, and added freshness to everything we saw. Emerging into what I would call a rural delight, farmers carting hay, and in distant fields tractors looking like toys in front of the massive grandiose Alpine backdrop. This was a little reminiscent of my home in Cumbria but on a much more magnificent scale. In this delightful ambiance we found a hostelry, converted from a convent on the outskirts of a village close to Bruck an der Mur.

It was time to take stock, not only of ourselves after the fast driving in Germany, but also of the van. Farooq busied himself checking the engine, he found a reason for the faulty steering, a bolt was missing which he deemed serious, but was able to rectify. He also changed the one remaining windscreen wiper to the driver's side.

The hostelry was just what we needed. Its overall simplicity, cleanliness and vaulted walls gave a feeling of safety and peace and we needed that. A woman who lived nearby came in and cooked, she was large, warm, friendly, and as wholesome and solid as her cooking and the place.

We allowed ourselves two nights of restorative sleep. I managed to write a long letter to my parents whilst we sat in a cafe in the town listening to heavy rain. I described the thunder echoing and re-echoing between mountains, to and fro, getting softer in the distance and then a sudden peal almost overhead. It made me think Beethoven must have been here! I mentioned this in the letter.

The following day we headed for Yugoslavia via Graz, and north of Zagreb, in the vicinity of Varazdin we digressed from the main route and found ourselves on narrow desolate roads which softly undulated. The sky was navy blue and every so often lit by flashes of orange or yellow sheet lightening. In this strangeness there was no rain, darkness was approaching quickly and early.

Fortunately, in the last embers of daylight, we chanced upon what one could call, an inn. Rustic in appearance, we had found a precious rarity almost as if caught in a time warp. There was utterly no self-consciousness about the quality of food or accommodation. I savoured the home cured pork and cold, white, dry, local wine, Farooq enjoyed a goulash-type stew.

Journeying on in the morning we enjoyed what we saw of Yugoslavian rural life, lightly golden tanned children with flaxen hair tending bronze coloured cows in idyllic countryside with pleasantly situated dwelling places in Slavonia. Much of the landscape appeared very inviting to settle in.

Further south continuing along main routes via Brod and Belgrade, we felt we were doing well when we reached 300 miles in a day, over that, we treated as a bonus. Crossing off kilometres on route maps, transferring them to miles was a preoccupation which later became an obsession on uninteresting and irksome roads.

We were into our journey a week, it was 12th August, when we arrived at the Bulgarian border with it's rude officials. This came as a abrupt shock after the friendliness in Yugoslavia, officialdom here appeared like something out of this world, not appertaining to it. Uniformed, booted, brusque men questioned whether we actually should be allowed in. We wondered whether we wanted in. Their rudeness made us apprehensive about what we might encounter in their country.

4

Bulgaria

Life goes on; we did not intend turning back at this stage. We swept along wide roads skirting heavily wooded mountains. It was from one such route that we took a turning to the left, just to retreat from the main thoroughfare briefly. Not a mile up the narrow, winding road we found ourselves in a village, nestled in a small clearing in a large forest. Obviously, this was a place geared for tourists with its multitude of gift shops.

In true surrealistic fashion we found an ultra-modern cafeteria, full of plate-glass and shiny tubular metal furniture. In the melange of the holidaying atmosphere, created by the visitors intent on enjoying every moment of it, we ordered our coffee. An agitated man, out of breath, hastily approached us and almost fell onto our table.

'Esperanto, Esperanto?' He gasped loudly. My affable companion invited him to join us, and conversing in limited French and Pigeon English we deduced that he had learnt Esperanto some six years previously and had not found even one person to whom he could converse in this enterprising language. His disappointment was apparent when he became aware that we too were not Esperanto literate. The disappointment turned to anger as he explained about the intention and the ideal, that there should be a common language for Mankind. Obviously this not having been realised, had left one sad and disillusioned man. However who knows, perhaps the next busload of tourists would include another Esperanto communicator. We wished him luck before a warm farewell and resumed our quest in the Morris.

I'm now unable to recall whether it was before, or after Plovdiv that we found a contestant for the 'World's Worst Toilet'. Back from the road on the left was a wooden hut obviously popular as a cafe, with the ground around worn bare. Beyond this was the edifice I needed. All were situated in a rather thin pine forest, and not only swarmed with the fervent tourists but this time wasps also.

About twelve feet from my intended destination, it was necessary to tread prudently to avoid stepping on large piles of human excrement. The nearer the building, the worse the stench and clouds of flies and wasps. Eventually I did arrive at the crude hole in the ground. Apparently it had been denied water for weeks if not months. Miraculously I successfully accomplished my mission and was not stung by the cloud of wasps and returned to Farooq. He waited well away from the scene and wisely declined braving the ordeal!

We stayed only one night in Bulgaria, this was in a modern hotel, robustly built in symmetric design on such a grand scale, it resembled a fortress. The corridors were straight, long and wide.

Wooden doors were of great weight, uniformity abounded even to the detail of internal fittings. Great care also had been taken with the furniture, which would take six men to lift, that its placement abide to the law of pure symmetry. Even the service was so official and cold it felt demeaning to ask for anything. It would be difficult to find a more appropriate set for a Kafka novel.

5

Turkey

Somewhat relieved to leave Bulgaria, into Turkey now, we continued our descent from the hinterland of Europe to the Mediterranean. The Sea of Marmara, which had tantalizingly glinted at us for what appeared to be a very long time, was now tangible. Our warm feet were soothed by its softly lapping warm water. Later, as we sat close by, we became overwhelmingly aware of the oven-like August heat.

Further along the coast we entered bustling Istanbul. The only quiet places which were apparent, were the mosques, and that was only when they were not being used for prayer. If ever there was an abundance of minarets and domes, it was here. The rest of the capital was crammed with people, to the point of overflow, and most appeared to be carrying something. Anything that possibly could be carried was, pipes, parcels in all sizes, sheep and goats. Shops, alleyways, streets, markets, and cafes with the pungent smell of spiced kebabs, all seethed with people and oozing sound, everyone doing, discussing, or arguing about something.

To escape from all this noisy activity we found a rather select western-style restaurant. We sat in the cool, air-conditioned, relatively spacious place, sipping black coffee and eating cream cakes. Cocooned in the order of the place I felt safe sitting by the window and viewing the chaos outside. With an elevated viewpoint we watched battered Cadillacs weaving and hooting their way through the shoals of people, we became mesmerised by a fat, little, khaki-uniformed man standing on a podium and having the impertinence to try and direct traffic!

His manner was restrained at first. Centrally placed, at the junction of five roads, he intermittently raised his baton and no one paid the slightest attention. Later his gesticulations became more pronounced and awkward. The noise and activity of the unconcerned drivers and people laden with goods continued relentlessly, and if anything, seemed to gain in momentum.

In this foray, as his light cloth covering his head, became wetter, he adopted whistle blowing as another tactic, then he singled out individual

motorists by pointing. His face had gradually became contorted. Without
warning and with a continuous blast of his whistle he briskly marched off
into the enveloping crowd and quickly disappeared. Had we been the only
people to notice that he had been there at all?

We finished our sweet Turkish coffee—I was partial to the black, thick
sediment at the bottom. Farooq and I gave each other a wry smirk and
left the cool place. The accommodation we found was in a rundown poor
area of the city, an extremely modest and not too clean boarding house.
But it did give us some respite from the bustle.

Unfortunately, as with many Westerners who visit Istanbul for the first
time, illness struck me with a vengeance. Not only was there the usual
Istanbul enteritis to cope with and the bladder infection returning, I had
quite severe abdominal pain which necessitated a visit to a doctor. He
diagnosed an internal infection and prescribed antibiotics, the injectable
sort, which in turn we had to buy from a chemist. This would involve
having to find a doctor each day to give the injection.

At this point, I had had enough and I wanted to go home. It was not
just the journey to Pakistan, which we were barely into by a third, with
the worst to come, but the journey back that concerned me. There also
was the fact that our meagre allocation of funds for accommodation
would not extend to a return trip.

In order to goad me, Farooq promised that he would arrange for me
to fly back from our destination and he would return with the van. For
the first time, in a long time, Farooq's dream of returning home was
becoming a distinct possibility. The goal was now tangible. His
disappointment by assenting to failure again would have been tremendous.
After a long debate it was only due to his promise that I relented. My
spirits had been lowered by infection and pain but they improved after
the first injection and three nights in the same bed actually helped.

We set off again, this time on the ferry from Europe to Asia. The cool
breeze from the Bosphorous blew refreshingly in our faces and knowing
we were leaving the frenzied activity of Istanbul behind gave me some
welcome extra strength.

We followed beside the pleasant Sea of Marmara for some time,
heading for Ankara some 287 miles away. Distances between main places
were increasing, with less happening in between. They also appeared less
accessible due to the falling standard of the quality of the roads. We
needed to take special note of petrol stations and use them when we
came across them.

At first, some time was spent, every day, looking for a doctor to give the daily injection. One was in a small village where men with jaundiced faces sat in the humble waiting room which was more like a cattle shed than a surgery. I knew the men were dying because their temples were hollow, and being a vet's daughter, I knew this had always been a death sign for a dog, at least.

To receive the injection in the surgery, I lay down on a bench covered in straw and prayed that the needle had been sufficiently boiled in water in order for it to be sterilized. In Ankara, I was much more fortunate as we managed to find a chemist which was modern and ultra clean. But stiffness after the injection was not helped by having to sit in the van all day, so I decided a jab every other day would have to suffice. In retrospect I now realise how foolish this was—chancing the infection returning in the middle of nowhere.

Passing through much barren, arid mountainous hinterland and long stretches of rough road, we were well aware the suspension on the Morris 1000 van left a great deal to be desired. It was with relief we arrived at the north coast of Turkey which also is the south coast of the Black Sea.

We thought we had arrived at the Promised Land! Boys were tending groups of goats and sheep among palm trees and with actual grass we felt surrounded by verdant green. Knowing that the Black Sea is inland added a peculiarity; the horizon was clear yet beyond was the coast line. The sea twinkled back at us in the strong sunlight almost winking and cows paddled to cool themselves. This reminded me of Holman Hunt's painting of a goat by the Dead Sea.

At the coast we turned right through Samsun and followed the narrow winding coast road, not too unlike the small road accompanying Wastwater in Lake District. Along the way we enjoyed the indigenous food which seemed a little like Pakistani fare but much more watery. Great use, in soups and curries, was made of the variety of local fish and freshly grown vegetables, especially green peppers and tomatoes.

Another feature, if you could call it that, throughout Turkey were the many rather elderly stout women, black gowned, with hooded appearance, trudging and stooping with large bundles of sticks stacked on their backs. They seemed to be all over the place, a bit like a scene from Monty Python. There they were coming round corners, struggling up hills. I don't think that I saw one member of the male population under such duress. Most of them seemed to be enjoying themselves lazing about cafes and drinking tea and many of the remaining appeared to be in the army, in equal lax fashion.

We left the coast road at Trabzon and wound up the Zigana Pass with hairpin bends. This climb was 6,600 feet above sea-level. Not far up our van cylinders started thumping loudly. We were barely half a mile from a garage where we had stopped earlier. Hearing the sound, Farooq immediately identified the problem, diesel instead of petrol had been put in the tank.

He was furious, and said that the mistake had been made due to me distracting him, which I am sure was quite true. Engine off, we backed down to the garage where he siphoned off the diesel swallowing some at the same time. When it was replaced with petrol, we didn't know just what amount of damage had been done to the cylinders in the engine.

After this pass, the next climb by Mt Kopdag was 8000 feet. The uncomfortable feeling of potential van failure and Farooq's jubilation at being in a Muslim country again shown by overtaking lorries, shoving his fist out of the window, and shouting, '*Mousalman*' at the top of his voice, had the effect of putting my nerves on edge. Although, I must say I felt recovered from the previous ailments. Driving on the right, overtaking on the left, meant I was directly above the drop sometimes of hundreds if not thousands of feet. Often a crumbling two foot stone wall was the only boundary between road and fall, and not even that was visible when you were close.

Ten years of not being in a Muslim country for Farooq must have been a very long time. It had taken a good part of Turkey before the penny dropped and he had started to feel more at home. He used his name 'Farooq' here; in Iran he was to use his first name, Mohammad. This, he said, was because of the different branches of Islam: the Sunni majority in Turkey acknowledged the Caliph Umar Farooq, while the Shia majority in Iran did not regard Umar Farooq as a Caliph at all. Umar Farooq was among the followers of the Prophet Muhammad (PBUH) and the Second in line after Muhammad (PBUH) to lead the early Muslim communities.

Farooq also used to tell me that in Arabic, a name of similar sound to my own, spelt *Haider* means the strength of Allah. This coincidence, while travelling with Farooq was in certain places very fortuitous for us, and we were greeted as very good news indeed.

One morning when we were still in this mountainous region, I recall a fairy tale landscape with little brown round-topped mountains and almost vertical sides, where we met a man who was so proud of his orchard that he invited us to have a breakfast of apples. This could not have been all fantasy because I took the photograph of Farooq standing alongside the man and his family posing in the orchard. The morning sunlight was broken into patterns by the shadows of the leaves, and the apples were shining red, juicy yet firm, and exquisite in texture and taste.

We continued heading for Erzurum, an important traffic point on the way from Ankara to Tehran and which contained a military zone, where cameras were forbidden. After that we traversed through barren hills and wanting to make up time, decided to press on into the night despite only one headlamp working. Half-way up a pass we were stopped by flashing and waving torches. Turkish gendarme explained that the road was too dangerous to travel in the dark and we were directed back to a sort of out-post, a small hamlet.

One of a group of boisterous men who had been drinking outside a cafe and who encircled the van on our arrival, opened the passenger door and almost dragged me from my seat toward the cafe. Farooq, for some reason, was not fully aware of this but he did sense the hostility and danger once we were inside. He became extremely annoyed by the overt rudeness and familiarity displayed by the men towards me. Thankfully, we just managed to retreat to our vehicle where we stayed locked in the entire night. We were too afraid to venture out, even to urinate.

The next day we made it over the pass to the Turkish-Iranian border and on the way regrettably missed views of Mount Ararat in the distance. From Istanbul to the Iranian customs I have given no idea of the ordeal of travelling every day in a Morris 1000 van over a distance of just under 1,200 miles. This is just Turkey alone.

We were now in a part of the world which was absolutely foreign to anything I knew or had experienced before. This was the threshold of a journey into the unknown.

On 21 August, our first night in Iran, we lay on jute-strung beds beside a resthouse, under the stars, myriads of them, awesome and fascinating. I thought, this is where the East begins. Peering up, I saw hosts of constellations, I'd never seen before. Observing the relationships and movement of sparkling, busy stars, made it difficult to think that sleep was of any consequence. But happily and eventually I must have dropped off.

6

Iran

It was on the road from Bazorgan, joint Turkish and Iranian Customs, to Tabriz, capital of Azerbaijan, in mountainous, hilly terrain that we were stopped again by khaki uniformed police. This time it was Iranian gendarme. There were three or four of them and they were accompanied by a camel whose height looked equivalent to a bungalows'. It looked dramatic, silhouetted in front of the soft, undulating sand dunes and pale sky. I was so taken by this, I disembarked to take a closer look, and then became aware of raised voices. Farooq demanded strongly that I return to the van, which although disappointed, I did. He then explained that the gendarmes were demanding to see his driving license!

Here we were in what appeared to be the middle of nowhere with no one else around. I had read about English travellers, who had been jailed by Gendarmes merely on suspicion of breaking the law in this very area. Attempting to avoid a very awkward situation, Farooq, in no uncertain terms told them, in Persian, to go to hell. There was a heavy sort of long quiet.

Very thankfully Farooq's bravado of bluff worked. He told me later that the gendarmes, had stopped us, only wishing to have a closer look merely because I was European and a female.

He also told me the reason why tarmacadam roads were fast becoming a thing of the past. This was due, he said, to the impossible task of building and keeping roads in desert areas as sand shifts so much. I could not help remarking about the numerous roundabouts. We could travel tens of miles on a straight road then suddenly there would be a roundabout, with no other visible roads joining the one you were on. We would circle then continue on the same road. Occasionally we would leave at a right-angle to our original route! I never did find out why, all I could surmise was that travelling was so boring that they were to offer relief to the tedium, or, in effect, stop the driver from going to sleep! Perhaps they were milestones in the desert helping travellers to pinpoint how far they had come.

The only other relief from tedium was found at resthouses or garages. One was by a couple of petrol pumps in a small village. The midday heat scorched through the metal van body, and made me feel like I was being cooked. I waited, soaked in sweat, as Farooq attended to the van's needs. Later, I wrote a rhyme as a description of the scene:

The Persian Fool

It was a place of sunlight
A garage in Iran,
When out of a shadowed corner
Came the voice of a small man.

His song spread round the village
It went down little lanes
It softly circled dwellings
Did the sweet voice of this man.

From out of the shadowed corner
Stepped the little old man
Dancing round and clicking!
Did the sprightly man.

Tilting forward slightly,
As he did his little steps.
He made his way towards me
I'm still sitting in the van!

Begging for some Dinar (Iranian currency)
For perhaps a cup of chai (tea)
Instead the garage attendant smote him
Full tilt right in the eye.

Stooping even further
I gave him his few Dinar,
He blest me straight from Allah,
Back to his corner skulked the man.

Another odd aspect of this occurrence was the fact that the clicking sound which emanated from him was most unusual. By some remarkable skill it looked as if his thumb became disjointed and the sound came from movement of bone on bone. His clicks were in perfect unison to his steps.

A little further on from the garage, Farooq was later to remind me, that wanting to kill kilometres, I hadn't wished to stop at Nishapur where the great Omar Khayyam was born, lived, 'busied' and died. I still regret this with shame as the *Rubaiyat* is a book I frequently return to and continues to give pleasure. It was also in the same area that, on an over night stay, Farooq translated the news on a radio. This was that the Soviets had occupied Czechoslovakia. From the Iranian broadcast it appeared that the Soviets had no alternative and were merely taking corrective action. It was explained to me that Iran was dependant on the Soviet Union for aid, and this incident revealed to me that a coin can be viewed from many different sides.

After a part-day and night stay in Tehran, where incidentally the multitude of roundabouts ran amuck, we headed for Mashhad—600 miles of very poor dirt road with little in between. A few tens of miles East from the capital, we stopped at a small hamlet, in reality a few thrown together huts.

As I looked out eastward and southward from the last hut, there were only layers of heat rising from the hot sand. The layers appeared to be changing level all the time, so if you looked for long enough, you became mesmerized by all the forms which could be read into the changing patterns and colours. In reality there was nothing there—the thought was chilling.

In this outpost we met a handful of young Germans who had been stranded for days. Due to a mishap they had no money and were unable to raise the fare for the weekly bus to Tehran. One fair-haired pleasant youth from Hamburg had sustained a nasty infected leg-wound. Using our first-aid kit and with no clean water available I managed, as best I could, to clean and dress the sore. I tried to explain that I had no medical experience, only that I had watched my father, a veterinary surgeon at work! This did not deter most of the villagers gathering round. All had various maladies I was unable to treat, even a blind man approached for help. Before leaving, we gave the Germans money for bus-fares for which they were extremely grateful. Who knows they could have been us, and for this reason travellers in such parts need to help one another.

Reliance on the resthouses and occasional petrol pumps sometimes separated by almost a hundred kilometres increased existing anxiety. On one occasion not long after filling up and not far into the day we realised from the petrol gauge that a mammoth amount of fuel had been consumed, and on checking the tank, found it leaking. This was probably due to stones flying up from the track and puncturing the metal. We had included fibreglass in our tool kit as a bit of an afterthought, and with its drying properties, enhanced by the heat, Farooq managed to do the repair. We marvelled about the stuff and the nature of it. Delays and wasting petrol were something we just could not afford.

Intermingled with anxiety about petrol and whether we would make it to the next pump or in daylight, there was just darned discomfort. Due to Farooq having installed a fan to cool the engine, what the fan did in effect, was drag the dust from the desert and fire it at our faces. Not only was it in our hair, clothes, eyes, noses and ears, but we ate it as well.

Furthermore, due to the loss of one windscreen wiper in Germany, sand drawn onto the windscreen piled upon the bonnet. This meant I could not see ahead so I crossed the desert blinded by the sand, as well as eating it. Farooq managed to see where we were going only due to his wiper working non-stop.

At the next resthouse, Farooq was unsure as to whether to sleep indoors. On his insistence, I sprayed our prospective beds with DDT. We also used our own sheets, being a little wary about the cleanliness of the place. This did not deter the bugs, which still successfully wheedled themselves through the beds and sheets. We awoke covered in swollen red welts and had the greatest of trouble ridding the blood-filled mites from our sheets and clothes. Water, not being a commodity readily available in these parts, made the task even more difficult and mainly manual.

It was at the self same place that the owner revealed he suffered from constant headaches, and all he dreamt about in life was having some Aspirin. No wonder, one may think, with all those bugs! We left him with a bottle more than half-full, and continued through the desert fighting the dirt, and now, irritation from the bugs.

At another resthouse we were met by a landlady's refusal to serve us. Partaking of the customary *chai*, usually served in a misty-coated greasy glass, was about the only comfort and friend in this desert of sand. The only other were the water melons. Farooq used to cut a little window through the skin then pulp the centre. The drink was always cool, refreshing and delicious. In our state of discomfort we were totally nonplussed by her refusal. She deemed us to be too dirty and pointed assertively to a stagnant pond, indicating by her actions that we should wash. On our returning, she could barely control her laughter.

'One brown, One white!' she exclaimed in broken English, 'We did not know! We could not guess!'

We were then welcomed into her tidy, clean home and were served royally. The plump-bodied woman went on to introduce us to her mother whose legs were swollen to a great size. Worried, our landlady quizzed us as to what ailment the old lady suffered from. Sadly, neither of us were able to enlighten her. She continued: 'I am thinking that perhaps I should sell my resthouse to pay for medical treatment' and further said that even advice was expensive. She was a warm generous person, not unlike some farmers' wives in the Lake District and it was apparent she took great pride in her resthouse. I hope something worked out for her. When we left we wished her well.

After another day or more of dust and heat, at Mashad we availed ourselves of a hotel with air-conditioning. We took an abundance of showers, and drank blended carrot and sugar cane juice bought from street vendors, and thought we were in heaven.

7

Mashhad to Kabul

On leaving Mashhad, we had another 152 miles of more partly gravelled, sometimes sandy and often pot-holed road to the Afghan border, Islam Quala. Darkness was almost upon us by the time we arrived. We had just been pre-empted by a coach load of Australians and the customs official told us that when he lit his paraffin lamp it was time to stop work. It was only after a great deal of lengthy persuasion he eventually stamped the Australians' then our passports. In frustration from this waiting ordeal of a couple of hours, and of course with darkness now totally upon us, we forgot to replenish petrol at the border.

It was well into the night when we ran out of fuel in the middle of what appeared nowhere. There was nothing more to be done than have a sleep upright, in the front of the van. We awoke in the early light probably due to discomfort. We surveyed the scene around us; perhaps two to three miles back in the arid, flat nothingness we saw a few dwellings raised on a small hillock and close to an outcrop of rock. From this hamlet, almost on the horizon, we saw a tiny speck of white.

We did not take much notice at first, then the speck appeared to gradually, grow larger. Having held our attention for some time, we then discerned that this speck was a person coming our way. After some time, a tall turbaned Afghan with white *kamiz* and grey *shalwar* presented himself and kindly invited us to share breakfast with him. Farooq was about to accept despite the walk back, when a black Mercedes, full of Pakistani men all wearing immaculate, dark suits, travelling in the opposite direction, stopped. We were greeted with salaams, as is customary, and asked very politely if we required any assistance. We explained our plight over the petrol and fortunately these people happened to be carrying a fuel can and appeared delighted to help. Furthermore, they would not entertain any remuneration from us.

Farooq still wished to honour the Afghan invitation, especially when the man had walked so far to deliver it. I rather callously insisted we should continue. We apologised and thanked the gentleman. He turned from us with great dignity to retrace his long steps back to his home. This incident did not please Farooq, who explained once again that to refuse hospitality can greatly insult the person offering it.

When we arrived in Herat we headed for the bank in order to exchange our money. Unfortunately, we were in for another long wait because the same Australians as those at the frontier had arrived just before us. There was nothing more to do but quietly queue behind. The visions of Afghanistan, as a wild and exciting part of the world, which I had gleaned from the Newby book, were dreadfully damaged by these trippers heading for Australia!

We set off again, this time on an asphalt road, newly reconstructed with Russian assistance, three hundred and fifty miles of it, to Kandahar. To relieve the hours of tedium, I attempted to increase my vocabulary of Urdu and Farooq tested me on the words. As he was doing me a favour I thought I would try to help him to improve his English in return. For example, the collective noun, but Farooq did not take kindly to this, tolerance for both of us was becoming a little stretched, so he continued to say 'hairs' for hair, and 'sheeps' for sheep and may well do so to this day.

At a welcome break by the road side, some Afghan men were adamant that I should photograph them. It took a while to get the exposure right using my Weston light meter. They were becoming impatient because I was taking so long, and Farooq sauntering about nervously in the background, told me to hurry. Some of the men appeared closer to seven feet rather than six. taking the photograph quickly, I hadn't noticed the little boy in rags standing behind the group until I made the print. I later learnt that child slavery in Afghanistan was common.

Arriving in Kandahar we hoped to find a better exchange rate for our pounds. We were directed and re-directed around an array of busy stalls selling exotic vegetables and fruit. Eventually, we found a trader to do the deal, these people seemed to thrive on argument about cost, expecting a quarter of an hour barter, even for something as insignificant as oranges, for there were plenty of them here. Farooq, to my mind did not haggle sufficiently and I told him off in no uncertain terms. He was becoming really sick of me and my nagging, finding fault wherever I could. The expression on his face said it all.

From Kandahar to Kabul we made good time on the 318 miles of, this time American assisted, Tarmac and asphalt road. Gaily painted large cattle trucks, often Bedford waggons, always fully laden, and with Afghan men hanging on at every available point, the ends of their turbans loose, flapping wildly in the wind, were commonplace.

We again became hopelessly intertwined with the Australians this time at the Khyber Restaurant in Kabul. It was the only western-style self-service cafeteria around, hence it's apparent popularity. The food, although described as continental, was wholesome and enjoyable with merely a slight oriental influence.

At a tailor's shop close to a bazaar, I ordered a suit, *kamiz* and *shalwar* with multitudinous rows of stitch-on cuffs at wrists and ankles. There was a delightful selection of cottons to choose from, in varied degrees of subtle non-colours and eventually I arrived at a type of khaki. While this was being made and aware that we had missed out on sight seeing on our trip, we decided to visit a place called Bamiyan, some 154 miles north-west in order to see some mammoth statues of the Buddha.

The night before our departure for the detour, whilst asleep on small metal twin beds in our hotel room, I jumped up thinking there was someone under my bed. Farooq also awoke with a start. Both our beds had lifted, what seemed like a foot in the air! Also we noticed the positions of our beds had changed. We learned the next morning that there had been an earth tremor, and later still, we learnt that this must have been the tail end of a number of earthquakes which had affected north Turkey and north Iran, roughly along the route we had recently taken!

8

Bamiyan

Most of the road to Bamiyan was like an old Cumbrian lane, grossly uneven, and similarly ambled on amidst pleasant scenery. Dissimilar was a meat shop on the right-hand side where a carcass was hanging, only shaded by sacks, and completely covered with wasps. Maybe the photograph I took was of incorrect exposure as it failed to reveal the wasps!

Shortly after this, we took a branch road to the left and followed a gorge. Far below men were risking their lives attempting to build a bridge across the rapids. These rivers from the Hindu Kush showed no mercy in their speed.

A few more miles of jolts along the stony lane, instead of fording a stream, to my horror Farooq chose to cross it by a bridge without side walls, which appeared narrower than the van itself. I closed my eyes and said a prayer. Fortunately our tyres did not overlap the edges sufficiently to cause problems. Farooq did not believe me when I told him. It was not until our return journey that he saw the actual width of the bridge and was utterly amazed that we had managed the crossing.

The nearer we came to our destination the more ancient, awesome and miraculous was the rock strewn landscape. The mountains loomed closer and larger, the darker it became. It was pitch black when we eventually found the Bamiyan Hotel and it was not until the morning that we could fully appreciate the place we had found.

Peace, if it exists on our planet, was surely here! The valley floor being very flat was intensively cultivated and adorned with lines of aspen trees. The greenness of it was accentuated by a porous pale cream rock on one side which rose like a wall from the base. Into the rock were carved two giant Buddhas, one 120 feet in height dating back to between the second and third centuries AD, and the other 175 feet from the third to fourth centuries. Around the Buddhas, little caverns made the rock look like a honeycomb.

After breakfast, as we stared up at one of the massive Buddhas, I read from a small handbook obtained in Kabul.

'Here in the drapery of these figures one recognises classic Greek folds, modified by local and Roman treatment.'

'This is not true.' Farooq said crisply.

'I'm only reading from a leaflet,' I explained demurely. 'How can you argue with that? I don't know anything about it, myself. I'm only reading what has been printed'

'These things were done like this long before in India.' He said vehemently. The clothes were just like this. The folds—just like this.' He waved his arm as if to accentuate the direction of the lines in the garment.

This indeed was unusual for him, prior to this I had never heard him speak strongly, never a bad word in my hearing at least. Although shocked, I still persisted and the issue developed into a full blown argument, and as it was the only real one we ever had, and in such a peaceful place, I still remember it. It makes me think now that it was significant that we were arguing over the artistic influences on the carving of a Buddha, about what belonged to the East and what to the West.

I still did manage to investigate some of the caves, much against Farooq's wishes, as the rock was crumbly and very soft. Each of the caverns had been used for Buddhist monks to meditate and were only large enough for a person to sit cross-legged. Each were of varying dimensions as if different monks required their own individual specific space in which to meditate. Some remnants of wall paintings were still visible, individualising the cells further. All were interlinked by a myriad of passages and tunnels much like a warren. Scrambling through a shaft with chunks of the powdery rock falling away, I was aware of Farooq's anxiety—it may just have been possible to fall into the mountain and not return! Also I was still hurt by our argument and I agreed to return with him to the hotel.

We showered and changed and even found a bar in the salubrious place. After travelling yesterday on inhospitable roads the hotel seemed unusual enough, but knowing that close by were two Buddhas said to have been carved just a few hundred years after Christ, it all seemed terribly incongruous.

Taking advantage of a little time—there had not been much on the journey which had largely comprised of travelling as far as we could in one day, then finding sustenance and rest—I read a little book by Nancy Hatch Dupree on Bamiyan. It appeared much of the history of the valley had been lost in the mists of time, but I did learn that for probably a thousand years, Bamiyan was a melting pot of ideas from West and East.

This was largely due to being an important rest place for rich caravans travelling between Balkh and Peshawar. Gold, and silver plates, wool, linen, glass vessels, wine and frankincense were some of the trade from the Roman Empire in exchange for rubies, furs, silk and gums from Central Asia and China.

The story goes that Genghis Khan had no intention of visiting the place initially, and sent his grandson. Unfortunately, the young man was killed, in 1222, near to the valley and close to the famous Red Fort, nearby. Genghis Khan was so enraged by this that he swore to put to death every living soul in the valley. It is said he came and he went, and left silence.

Islam also possibly played a part, because of lack of tolerance of religious images most of the faces of the Buddhas had been hacked away. But another theory was that at one time there had been jewels in the eyes and thieves were responsible for the vandalism.

We were musing about the Buddhas, in the bar, when a tall dark moustached, gangly man introduced himself to us. He was not a native of Bamiyan, but he had been in the village for some time, as its bank manager. He had a certain yen to visit some lakes, at Band-i-Amir, about 50 miles further up the road. He said the lakes were exceptionally blue, said to be the bluest in the world! Farooq, always willing to oblige a total stranger, agreed and we would start in the morning. I was happy, sufficiently fascinated by the 'blue'!

9

Band-i-Amir

We had tried to explain the difficulty about the fan collecting dust and firing it back at us, to our passenger, but this had not deterred him at all. He obviously had not grasped the full significance until he suffered first-hand. He was rather surprised that it was so bad and complained at length. He then partially solved the problem by tying a red spotted neckerchief around his nose, much like cowboys, and bandits. I will call the gentleman Mr K., because he wished to remain anonymous for reasons I will disclose later. Sitting in the front, on our 50-mile trip west of Bamiyan, in a dusty white Morris, on lanes deteriorating by the mile, the bank manager, resembling more a villain, must have cut a pretty sight.

Our major problem en route evolved about three miles from our destination. There was such a steep climb that the van could not make it to the top. Luckily our hand brake was effective, halting our descent each time we were obliged to back down. The worry I had was that even if we did make it to the top, what about the drop at the other side of this pass? What if we couldn't make it back? In our literature it said that the place was totally cut off by snow in winter months.

On the third attempt Farooq decided to have a really good run at the pass. Fully accelerating in low gear prior to the ascent this time, we were lucky and just made it to the top. The view immediately rewarded our efforts. A pale undulating landscape, interrupted by porous rock-cliffs and scree stretched out for miles and miles into the distance.

Down below was the lake, it certainly was very blue. Dark ultramarine, contrasting with the surrounding bleached silver sand and very strangely the sky was a very pale egg shell blue only interrupted by the occasional small cloud. In other words, the lake owed nothing to the sky and its reflection, for its intense colour. The descent was very steep indeed, we wound around the hairpin bends which almost doubled back on themselves as we crawled on down.

Remarkably, at one end of the lake the water was about fifteen feet higher than the immediate ground around. It was cupped in by a wall of rock acting as a natural dam. At its rim, water lapped over and ran down the wall staining it in a multitude of mineral colours, such as copper, chrome yellow and veridian.

Almost at the far end of the lake was a mosque which was said to have been built in honour of Allah's hand, which had formed the lake by cupping it and then leaving it with the boundary wall. According to Mr K. no one actually knew how the water had come to the place. There weren't any signs of streams: but one theory was that this was spring water.

Certainly the water was pristinely crystal clear, and through it could be seen an abundance of plant life. This alone was a fascinating sight. We made our way to the mosque, outside of which was a small tent. We were welcomed by a slightly built man, stooping and offering us victuals.

The only manifestation of any food source around were hens scratching about looking for sustenance in the arid ground. It was, therefore, not surprising that the only item offered was an omelette. We sat sipping our customary *chai* cross-legged, enjoying the tent's shade and waiting to be fed.

Mr K. expressed his delight on being here, also his gratitude for our bringing him. We were equally delighted and grateful to him for suggesting it, and a friendship had been struck. When the omelette arrived, brought by the same man who was also the keeper of the mosque, feeling famished, we devoured all, despite its strange odour and peculiar taste. The cost of this victual could have been interpreted as excessive, but as it may well have been the only food in a thirty mile radius we were more than fortunate to have partaken of it, or so we thought at the time.

It wasn't until much later that the omelette caught up with us with ensuing dysentery. We had been tired and it was late when we had arrived back in Bamiyan to find the hotel full. Mr K. had offered us the floor of the bank for us to sleep on. It is for this very reason that he wished to remain anonymous. Mr K. was no ordinary bank manager, he had been employed to investigate corruption and fraud in banks throughout Afghanistan.

Bamiyan was merely one of many banks in which he had resided. He insisted that we should give him our word never to speak to journalists about the matter of us sleeping in the bank, or perhaps his position would be untenable. I am breaking the trust now because Mr K. would have been in his fifties when we met him. I am presuming he will be well-retired today, and well beyond any recrimination. Despite the floor being hard and the bowel discomfort, we were still mightily grateful for the honour of being trusted to sleep safely, locked in a bank.

IO

Kabul to the Frontier

Back in Kabul, after our detour of about 400 miles, I collected my finished suit, which was beautifully made, and I was greatly delighted. By now we had been, on the road, so to speak, for four weeks. Merely 155 miles intervened between us and the Pakistani frontier, Torkham. The road was described in our A.A. route guide as tarmac, so we thought, little divided us from Pakistan.

It was, therefore, still reasonably early in the day when we arrived at the border situated at the foot of the Khyber pass. Which brings me back to the time when the customs was rather unwilling to let us through to our destination. Darkness had fallen long ago when the custom's official finally acquiesced and stamped our passports. He then slowly leaned back in his chair.

'U-n-f-o-r-t-u-n-a-t-e-l-y,' he said dragging out the word as if to give it extra weight, 'You will need to stay here, it is too dangerous to continue at night. There is tribal warfare, and it is not unknown for white people to be kidnapped and disappear.'

We had little option. Farooq was relegated to the barracks and as I was the only female on the encampment, the front of the van was deemed safest. An armed sentry was positioned at the van's side where he stood presumably to guard me through the entire night.

When I awoke the next morning, it seemed the same man was still standing there. This time, thank goodness, we managed to make an early start. Firstly through ancient rock landscape and then meandering down a zigzagging road from the Khyber Pass we passed by small hamlets of croft-like dwellings. The difference to the Scottish versions were the doors which resembled those in saloons in the Wild West. Also appropriate to the doors and dissimilar to Scotland, were the huge men standing by them, with large bullets strung on wide leather thongs around their chests, and each grasping a large heavy rifle. This certainly wasn't a place to stop, we thought, glancing at each other as we sped on down.

Gradually the rock landscape with the inhospitable hamlets evolved into more accommodating environs. The road still descending, we were enveloped in greenery and great beauty. Like an English garden but with no artificial boundaries. It appeared to stretch for as far as the eye could see. Rhododendrons, cyclamens, touches of vivid flower hues, in verdant green, and within all this, in the distance an azure lake beckoning.

As we gathered momentum down the straight road, we saw a man alighting from a tonga some two to three hundred yards ahead. Because the tonga was situated on the other side of the road, we didn't take a great deal of notice, at first. Then the man, with his back toward us commenced crossing over at a very slow pace. We were nearly on top of him, when Farooq applied the brakes. By the time we managed to stop, the man was almost leaning on our bonnet.

He waved a stump of a leg in the air with a circular motion. One of his arms shielded his one light blue wall eye, the other socket was closed, the eye missing. His other arm firmly embraced a heavy stick used as crutch and stave.

'He's blind,' I gasped, feeling dreadfully sorry for him. To say the least both of us were shocked by the abrupt encounter. It was only good fortune that the brakes had worked effectively and we hadn't mowed the him down.

He sidled nervously to my side of the van rather like a shy, and in retrospect sly, dog. He then held his hand out as if to receive alms. I had wound the window down and fished out a rupee, worth about one and a half shillings. He took the note, then placed his hand on my head as if to bless me. The next moment he grabbed my shoulder. Angered and embarrassed, I was about to get out, and belt him with his stave. Farooq set off so quickly that the van leapt forward like an antelope. I explained somewhat unnecessarily what I had intended, and Farooq explained that the man would have killed me if I had tried.

'A person like that is stronger than you can imagine,' he said.

It took time to realise that the whole pantomime had been staged from beginning to end. We thought the man had not seen us when disembarking, and crossing with his back to us. His timing had been immaculate, a little sooner it may have been ineffective, a little later perhaps fatal. This was a feat of much practice and calculation.

He probably did it all day, every day and found it worthwhile to reimburse the tonga driver. Or perhaps who knows, the beggar could have owned the tonga and employed the driver. One aspect he could not have calculated, was the condition of our brakes. The man had risked his

life for a rupee. I asked myself if we had equivalent men in the West. I
certainly didn't know of any. He was the first Pakistani, apart from the
customs official, that I had met in his own country and he certainly was
an introduction.

Part Two

II

The Arrival—Home

We paid a toll to cross the Ravi Bridge into Lahore. Looking downstream to the right, I saw an island in the middle of the river, and on it was what looked like an empty villa. On the Lahore bank to the left of the bridge were extensive nomadic settlements. All conceivable items from plastic to wood were used to make improvised shelters.

Into the city we passed by one of the largest mosques in the world, the great Badshahi Mosque. Its deep red sandstone alleviated by lines and designs in white marble glistened iridescently in the sharp sunlight. As we headed for Mochi Gate, close to the ancient walled city, and Chamberlain Road, Farooq's home, I remarked on the numerous Morris 1000 cars. Farooq said that some of them were thirty years old or more.

I also marvelled at all the activity around, black buffaloes tethered and feeding, massive white bull buffaloes pulling cartloads of large rolls of newsprint weighing tons, rickshaw drivers pipping high pitched horns, thin, tired horses pulling tongas. Pakistani men dressed in off-white weaved their way through this on bikes. Then there was the noise, of Punjabi music, chatter, sheep bleating, buffaloes braying that accounted for only some of the cacophony. Also, everyone seemed to have a job here. There weren't many offered, so people created them, however menial. I was later to see that there were people who supplied rickshaw drivers with drinks of water, and that was their job exclusively, and boys collected bottles to return to appropriate places. If there was a possible need, there was always a job to fill it.

When we, at last, arrived at Farooq's home many of his family members were there to greet us. We sat in their sitting/reception room whilst they were unpacking their individual gifts. Rehana, an older sister, and Dr Aftab, a brother, and some of the children had eyes like bottomless, light brown pools. They looked with great love on the simple items we had brought, towels for Dr Aftab, Oil of Ulay and cosmetics for Rehana. Ghazali, thin and small for his two and a half years, treated his two dinky cars with reverence.

There was so much warmth here. They were overjoyed to see Farooq after the ten year absence, and because I was with him, I too was welcomed. Their acceptance, love and hospitality given on this first occasion amazed me, and made me feel that I had arrived home. It was not only restorative after the journey, but restored my belief in the goodness and kindness of human nature. Even today I still find it a useful reminder.

Farooq's four sisters lived in Lahore, three of them being at home in the apartment. They were, Lily, Rehana and Lubna. Only two, Javed and 'elder brother', of his four brothers still lived at home. Elder Brother, as he was called, had recently lost his wife during the delivery of their sixth child. The sisters at home had taken on the care of the baby and the rearing of the other five children. Lubna, Farooq's third sister, while she was still a baby, had fallen from the first floor balcony and remained with partial paralysis down her right arm and left leg, and although having difficulty with her education, persevered in studying at home. The eldest sister had left home and lived in another part of town with her husband and children.

The first floor rented accomodation consisted of three rooms and a bathroom linked at the front by a balcony overlooking the street. At the back was a walled, dirt-floored square yard. Upstairs, linked by another dirt floored open yard was a small toilet at the near end, and at the far end, a brick building in disrepair, which Dr Aftab sometimes, when at home, used for his studies.

The frugality of their home was a great shock to me at first, especially when compared to the standard of ours in London, which although was not excessive in England, appeared so here. Perhaps my shock was apparent, because it was suggested that we stay with Mr and Mrs Rafique and family in Canal Bank, a residential upper class modern part of town.

The situation at the Rafique's home was very different. It was quiet, there were no cries from street vendors, loud music from transistors, or the sound of the frenzied activity of the tonga drivers, buffaloes and sheep. There were also servants to wash pots and pans, to cook, to clean and to wait on every whim. I felt rather uncomfortable with this service, those who served having such low status as if they did not feature at all.

I am not saying that the Rafiques treated them badly. Genteel Mrs Rafique came from a very upper class family and Mr Rafique, I think at that time, was about to, or had just retired from being an official on the Railways. His English was impeccable, and we had corresponded prior to making the trip. He was a long standing friend of Farooq's and someone Farooq respected. I would describe him as highly intellectual though somewhat impractical at times. He and his wife eventually became valued friends of mine also.

But apart from not liking their attitude toward the servants, which would be commonplace for higher middle-class people, and was unquestioned, it was not pleasing to see this attitude extend to their children. Having met Farooq's brother's children they were worlds apart. And although grateful for our stay it was difficult to come to terms with, especially when I was aware of the lifestyle of Farooq's family and also where I felt more at ease and at home. After a few days, we returned, against Farooq's wishes as the Rafiques were the last people in the world he would want to offend.

Back at Farooq's home, the time was well used helping with chores and getting to know the five delightful children, baby Anse, and the rest of the family. Ghazali, meaning deer eye, was well-named and his assistance well appreciated. A two and a half year old finding a shovel to sweep dirt onto, in my country was completely unknown to me, but Ghazali amazed me by doing so. Indeed, all the children seemed greatly wise and mature for their chronological ages.

The chores were not aided by many modern facilities, items we in the West took for granted were absent. The sweeping in the home usually involved squatting and using a bunch of reeds and the cooking was done on paraffin stoves, ours being a welcome addition, which meant there were now two.

The bathroom was around six foot square, cemented and unpainted, and had lukewarm water which came from red hose pipes. I later learnt it was lukewarm, because of the Artesian wells which serve Lahore. Two buckets were in the room with some cans, which were used to ladle the water over oneself.

The toilet on the roof, a small brick building, had a wooden seat supported on either side with bricks and underneath the round hole was a porous bowl. Also in the edifice was a little fluorescent lime green lizard with shocking pink eyes who appeared whenever you went there. Every few days a friendly woman, who must have had a large soul because her sense of humour prevailed, came to empty the bowl. She had become a

Christian, having formerly been a Hindu from the Untouchable caste. She took the excreta away in a sack. I was told that this was usually dried and used as fuel for burning.

Having described all that, there was electricity in the flat despite the crude old wiring, but that is when it was on, power cuts being frequent. Often for long periods in the afternoon, when the fans were most needed, we sat, myself wet with perspiration. Everyone else appeared dignified and cool, but no doubt we all longed for the electricity to return.

There was also one washing machine in the vicinity. This was owned by a handsome looking woman, a neighbour who lived just behind the apartment at the back. She was already well known for grinding her own grain and could be seen working from time to time, with a large pestle and mortar on her flat roof, behind.

The washing machine reminded me of the early fifties back in England when my father bought a television which was unusual at the time as there were few in our immediate vicinity. For the Queen's Coronation many friends and neighbours congregated in our sitting room to view the spectacle. In Lahore, fifteen years later, a washing machine had the same novel fascination.

Two rows of about six wooden seats were placed facing the machine in order for the onlookers to be accommodated. Some local women brought their sewing, others merely found a focus for a chat, but most stayed for some time in order to view the entire programme! Farooq's family, by the way, did not, in fact, ask any favours from the woman with the machine but usually had a *dhobi*, who collected some garments each week and returned them, washed and ironed a few days later.

At night-time, with about thirteen of us in the flat at any one time, we used the entire apartment for sleeping, including the study and yards. There were many more people than beds so some slept on the floors. The beds were strung with jute and had lathed legs to make it difficult for snakes to crawl up. Usually, the electricity remained on during the night, and if you were beside a fan in one of the yards, looking up at the stars, this was delight indeed!

12

Family

The rhythm of life was so slow in Lahore it was almost impossible to keep a grip on time, it slipped and lapsed. All of Farooq's brothers came across as strikingly individualistic and utterly different from each another, both in appearance and in their specialities. Elder Brother, a headmaster and donning as many degrees as children, was a devout Muslim. He and I often found ourselves wishing to use the bathroom at the same time. Ablutions being a prerequisite prior to prayer at the mosque. This involved three visits during daylight and once at an unearthly time in the morning and once just after dark.

I seldom covered my head indoors to show respect for others, as is customary, with the *dupatta*, a type of chiffon scarf. To counteract, if you like, my wanton actions, at that time, I believed Elder Brother would wear a towel over his head. Our little ritual bordered on the ridiculous, especially when repeated so often. He would pop his head around the door of his room, looking furtively in quick nervous glances around the edges of his towel, then, if I was making for the bathroom too, make a quick towelled retreat! Looking back at this now, I think Elder Brother probably wore a towel over his head anyway and it was nothing to do with me, my customs, or lack of them.

On the other hand Javaid, the student, did not attend the mosque, but was politically orientated and spoke English as if he had swallowed an old book of English colloquialisms.

'My English is very rusty, what is that saying? An ill wind brings no good? Is that how you say it? There is trouble in Northern Ireland, it is very serious. What do you think about Northern Ireland?'

'There is always some trouble in Ireland.' I replied, fobbing him off with a quick reply. He had approached me on this occasion in the kitchen area next to the bathroom where I felt it was hardly conducive to become entrenched in talk. We normally conducted any discussions upstairs in Aftab's old study. Anyway, I was largely unaware of what was happening in the world then, with hindsight I now know Javaid was referring to the rumbling of the beginning of the violent dissent which has plagued Northern Ireland almost ever since.

The discussions we had on the roof were always attentively listened to by one, usually Bilal and a few of the other children, standing wide eyed. Bilal the eldest, his name meaning the crier from the minaret who calls people to prayer, was also attentive to any needs we may require such as tea. Ghazala his sister, her name being the female version of deer eye, helped Lubna downstairs with the fulfilling of any of these requirements.

Javaid explained to me about the many and varied political parties in Pakistan. He wished, like many people I met, for his country to become a true democracy. Under Ayub Khan, he said that not everyone had a vote, and the system was loaded in favour of keeping power and government among family and friends.

From time to time, I used to observe in the flat, piles of small leaflets appearing then disappearing and sometimes for periods of days Javaid too would disappear. Often when Lily, Rehana and I were out and about in Lahore, we spotted Javaid in different parts of the city on his bicycle intent on going from one place to another. I remember asking Lily, how often Javaid was expected at College. I think she replied: 'Javid has so many interests.'

These outings of the three of us often took hours to arrange and sometimes days. I recall thinking it was remarkable that anything got done at all. There was so much preparation with clothes alone, before leaving the house. All would be ironed, Rehana and Lily preparing not only their own shalwar, kamiz, dupattas, and the children's clothes, but mine also. For special occasions silk saris were ironed impeccably. And if there was an electricity cut the old iron heated by placing hot cinders inside, would be their only tool. On top of all their beautiful clothes sometimes they would cover themselves with the customary black *burqa*, coat and veil. Once I remarked in jest,

'How on earth will I recognise you? You seem to disappear behind those veils!'

They thought this was amusing. I suppose a *burqa* can be useful if you wish to travel incognito, a better disguise was never invented. We often used to frequent Anarkali Bazaar looking for gifts for me to take back. I was fascinated by the fine silver filigree jewellery and enjoyed comparing the different qualities from shop to shop. Another delight in the Bazaar were the cafes. They sold only one item, and that was fruit *chaat*.

This dish is made from seasonal fresh fruits such as, melons, grapes, bananas, other more exotic fruit, and often chick peas. Very special spices are sprinkled and mixed with the fruit; chilli powder, salt, freshly ground black pepper, being some of them. All this is then drenched in fresh lime juice and a little sugar. The fruit is allowed to absorb the juice and spices and in these small cafes you can choose between having the dish chilled, or at normal room temperature. Usually the cafe consisted of a small room with a bench around, over the doorway would be strips of gaily coloured plastic allowing the breeze to enter, and there would be a fan buzzing overhead. As havens of cool, such places were desirable enough, but serving this delicacy as well, they were out of this world!

13

Lahore Fort and Mausoleums

Being on holiday and visiting Lahore for the first time meant to some extent being treated like a tourist. Although visits to the bazaar were informal and part of every day life in Lahore, there was a formal tourist trail which was thought to be essential for the visitor. I certainly didn't feel like a tourist on holiday, especially after the trip of more than six thousand miles. But since we had actually, successfully, miraculously arrived at our destination, places of historical interest in the city were on my itinerary at least.

Lahore is situated to the north-west of the Indian subcontinent, on the banks of the Ravi, one of the five tributaries of the Indus and in the fertile plain of the Punjab. Its strategic placement can only be rivalled by Delhi. Further east is the vast two thousand mile long plain linking the Indus valley to the Ganges. All travellers and invaders from the North and West would have found Lahore a place of significance. The Aryan, Mughal and British Empires are three of the dynasties to touch the city and leave their mark. Seeped in these legacies from the past, Lahore Fort, if not the most significant of these, was an obvious first port of call.

Although the site dates prior to the sixteenth century, it was the Great Mughal Emperor Akbar who ordered it to be rebuilt and walled the town. It was added to and altered during the next five centuries, amongst others by Emperor Jehangir who erected royal mansions, and his son Shah Jahan who demolished them to have space for his own. For some reason, Farooq and I were to make this visit alone.

We entered by a vast fortified gateway opposite the Sikh tomb of Maharaja Ranjit Singh with gold-coated domes. The walls of the fort were mammoth in thickness and we followed through great gates to a grand stairway. The stairway steps and the gates had been especially designed for elephants! One could imagine the Emperor with his paraphernalia seated, canopied on a decorated elephant mounting the grand steps curving up past the foot of the eunuch's balcony, by the sheer scale of the place. The eunuchs attended and waited on the ladies of the harem, and

I expect would have watched the procession. For us mere pedestrians, the steps, because of their scale, were quite an awesome climb.

At the top, we found ourselves on the brow of a small hillock and at one end we saw where emperors had reclined on a raised dais, bordered by a low, marble fret-worked wall. Farooq explained that this would be where people would congregate and ask favours, help or advice. Scenes like this are brought to life by the Mughal miniatures, great examples of which I later saw in the Lahore Museum.

After musing on such things we were beckoned by an attendant who lit a paraffin soaked rag which was wound around the end of a short thick stick. We were ushered into one of the chambers of the Palace of Mirrors, Shish Mahal. This was made up of small concave mirrors on faceted walls not unlike a miniature chapel in regard to its architecture. The man spun the flaming rag around and amazingly the myriad of twinkling reflections from the light was the nearest artificial creation of an eastern night sky I have ever witnessed. The experience was breathtaking, and returning home in the dying light by tonga, Farooq and I felt the whole experience had been uplifting.

Dusk was always the right time here to return home, it was the most beautiful time. There was a feeling of sadness and that you were witnessing transience and greatness, as the air grew heavy with the aroma of blossom, and it felt like souls floated about giving even more pathos to the atmosphere.

Sometimes at this time of day, Dr Aftab and I would talk for hours. They were the sort of conversations I had never experienced before. Westerners have a habit of putting what is said into compartments and relating it to their own experiences and themselves. There was no restriction like that here. Ideas developed and because they weren't contained, restricted or restrained were allowed to develop in space as they almost turned in the air. It was possible to view everything at different angles and toss the abstract form around beyond and above our heads seeing it in various concepts of time.

Perhaps this is one of the differences between Easterners and Westerners. Another being that many Easterners lack the abrasive personas found in Western cultures and I believe because of this, I felt comfortable with Pakistani people long before coming to Lahore.

Another memorable outing was with most of the family to the Mausoleums of Emperor Jehangir and his beloved Empress, Noor Jehan. Set in vast gardens just outside the city, there was a great feeling of peace. We sat on a grassy bank, in a more informal part of the garden, close to the Empress' Mausoleum where workmen were busy restoring the three hundred year old marble mosaics. Long lengths of pale pink marble, resembling the shapes of letters in the making of Blackpool rock, small sections of which were being gently filed to make segments to replace gaps in the intricate designs on the Mausoleum's flooring. The craftsmen told us that this was the way the mosaic had been done originally.

Sitting to rest our legs in the heat, I observed groups of men talking together under clumps of trees in rather plain, old fashioned cream western suits. It was how I had imagined it was before the First World War in our country and I felt there was an innocence about it which somehow had not been interrupted by two world wars.

We hadn't made arrangements to eat. This was rarely necessary in this part of the world, which the following may prove. Here we were sitting on the grass, out of town, no restaurants, when virtually from what seemed like nowhere, behind one of the bushes, a boy popped up, and asked us what we would like to eat. We ordered rice, *chappatis*, a selection of curries, in short, a feast. To my amazement, after some time all these things appeared before us and were laid out like a royal picnic in this delightful setting!

When we returned home, Lubna, who was extremely attentive in the nicest of ways, continued to wait on my every whim. I respected and loved her greatly. A mere suggestion of tea and it would be there, and anyone who knows me knows how much I like tea, and here it was of especially fine quality. I had never tasted anything like it before—not having to cross two continents before arriving on the table, improves it somewhat. With her care and attention, and being grateful if she picked up a snippet of English for her service, I was spoilt as I never had been.

14

Aftab and Nankana

Because Farooq's parents were no longer alive, Rehana acted as the female head of the family with the support of her younger sister Lily. Not only were these two largely responsible for the upbringing of their eldest brother's six children, they were also expected to act in other matters regarding their other brothers' welfare.

One such matter was a marriage for the Doctor. Whether Aftab asked the two sisters on his behalf to arrange a marriage or the two sisters had decided that a marriage would be good for him, or whether it was merely traditional in these circumstances, is not clear. But it was clear that all parties involved were keen to resolve this affair. The sisters were favourably disposed to one of their old school friends as a potential bride.

I didn't think it a good idea for me to be involved, but Aftab insisted that I should meet this young lady and let him know what I thought. I knew that I would have difficulty being objective about this. For one thing, I was not too sure if the sister's desire to have their friend as part of the family was as much for themselves as for the Doctor, or whether indeed, this mattered. Another element in this was that I had grown fond of him myself. I didn't convey these thoughts to any of them.

Before arranging this meeting, Aftab wished to return to his practice in Nankana Sahib and he wanted Farooq and I to accompany him. We used our van for the 20 mile or so journey, and I sat in the front between the two brothers.

Once we were out in the country we came across small settlements of nomads. Aftab and I expressed a romantic view of nomadic life, being able to move on to a fresh tomorrow, leaving the cares you don't wish to have behind. In reality, I am sure much nomadic life is driven by necessity and I doubt if the element of choice enters into it much. Then, however, I preferred the idea of a carefree existence.

We stopped at a level-crossing in order to let a massive hissing steam train pass. Men were shovelling gravel from a tender onto the embankments on the sides of the line. The noise of gravel hitting other gravel and the loud sound of the gleaming pistons of the engine contrasted rudely with the rather rural idyllic setting in which we were placed. The three of us watched and listened transfixed, as the monster slid past.

Arriving at Dr Aftab's house, situated on the one long dusty main street of the busy small town, Nankana, was like arriving at a perfectly decorated, ornate, iced cake. The fine fret work on the balcony and balustrade around the flat roof, which had final embellishments of ornate urns at the corners, were all white and all gleaming brightly in the sunshine.

To the left of the Doctor's surgery and waiting room on the ground floor, we ascended by narrow steps to his apartment on the first. This consisted of two small rooms linked by a balcony at the front and on which was an old water pump. Not too unlike the layout of the Lahore flat but on a much smaller scale and instead of the three rooms, two. A small yard with steps led to the flat roof with toilet.

We were met in the apartment by two beautiful village boys who, I was to find, were always hanging around keen to run errands for the Doctor. I also met Farooq's fourth brother, Zulfiqar who appeared very warm, friendly and interesting.

We talked well into our first night. Zulfiqar and Aftab wanted to know all about England and my friends, and what they did, and what they were like. Aftab played some music on his home-made instrument which was a bit like a cross between a sitar and violin but with only one string. I have never heard such nuance from a single string. He also sang some Punjabi folk songs, one of them being:

> *There is no use crying over spilt milk,*
> *The cat has eaten the cream!*

Another song was about the one love in a man's heart which he carries until death. It was explained that although the man may marry someone else, it is the love in his heart who he is together with in heaven. A deeper meaning persists for me but whether it was there at the time I'm not totally sure.

Aftab, whose name means the sun, also managed to play the tabla very adeptly. He certainly impressed me with his varied talents. Very late into the night, I suggested that perhaps it would be nice to go for a walk. Aftab, in his quiet polite English said: 'I would have arranged it if I had known. It is necessary to arrange these things beforehand, because it would be necessary to have a tonga, and the driver needs some warning, and it is too late now. I asked why we couldn't just walk. He replied. 'It is too dangerous to walk at night because of rabid dogs, they are mad and they bite.'

The next day Farooq and I went to visit the Sikh temple not far from the doctor's house. Aftab had described a 'Book which was of great holiness to the Sikh's'. At certain specific times during the day, he had explained, the Book would be moved to a different position in the room where it was kept.

Unfortunately, when we arrived at this particular room we found it to be locked. I stood on tip toe stretching to peer through the partly shuttered barred windows, a glimpse of this fascinating evasive manuscript would have been enough. This was not to be and was a great disappointment, but we resolved that we would return at another time.

The temple at Nankana Sahib holds special reverence for the Sikhs because Guru Nanak, the founder of their religion, was born in the town. The story I was told about the Guru by Aftab went like this: 'Possibly partly because the Guru's beliefs were somewhere between Muslim and Hindu and he relied on both religions as a source of his faith, when he died, his body disappeared. Both Muslims and Hindus could have laid claim to his corpse. As it was, it was possible to divide his shroud into two and satisfy the claims by Hindus and Muslims. Half the shroud went to the Muslims and half to the Hindus. The beliefs of Sikh's, I was told, 'do not recognise this as a solution to a practical problem, but interpret these happenings as having great religious significance.'

Back at Aftab's home we enjoyed the cooking of Zulfiqar. In the afternoon, Zulfiqar dressed up as a kind of Pierrot for me to take photographs especially to give to an art student friend in England. I had spoken to him about her, and due to the fact that she enjoyed paintings of French clowns, especially Pierrot, Zulfiqar obliged.

Aftab later, after surgery, introduced us to some of his friends. One being a furniture maker, another a silversmith, we looked at a table in the making which was inlaid with small leaves of imitation ivory. Aftab said he would like to give it to me when it was finished and Farooq offered to bring it back to England in the van. From the silversmith Aftab purchased an ashtray, silver plated in the form of a heart which was also to be a gift.

After a delightful further day, meeting more friends of the Doctor's and taking more photographs, Farooq and I returned to Lahore leaving Zulfiqar and Aftab in their village. We hadn't managed to return to the

Sikh temple on this occasion. But for me, whatever kind of time we had away from the family and children in Lahore, it was always good to return.

Austrian landscape with cross

Farooq mending the van (Bruck an der Mur)

Golden tanned children tending cows (Yugoslavia)

Cow by the Black Sea I

Cow by the Black Sea II

After a breakfast of apples, Turkey

Men posing with slave boy,
Afghanistan

Kabul Market

Meat shop,
Afghanistan

Building a bridge on the way to Bamiyan

Bamiyan Buddha

On the road from Bamiyan to Band-i-Amir

The blue lake

Band-i-Amir, lake cupped
in by boundary wall

Water lapped over staining the wall

The water was pristinely clear.

Tea at Band-i-Amir, Farooq with Bank Manager

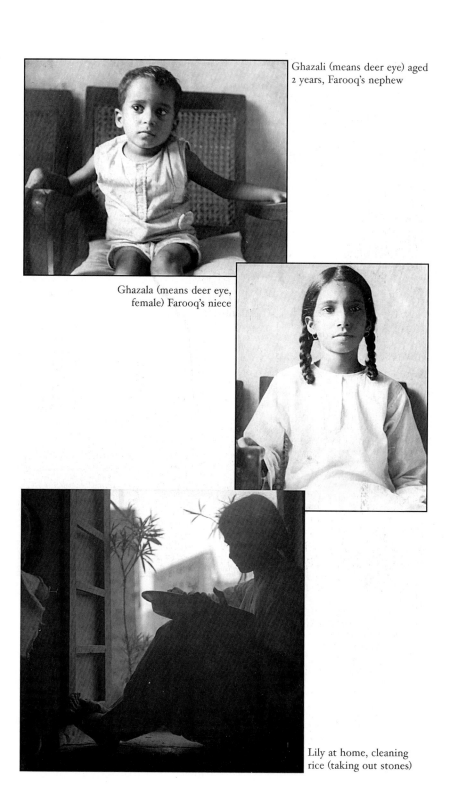

Ghazali (means deer eye) aged
2 years, Farooq's nephew

Ghazala (means deer eye,
female) Farooq's niece

Lily at home, cleaning
rice (taking out stones)

Dr Aftab's house

Zulfiqar as a Pierrot

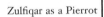

Family in Nankanasahib

Mr Choudri's mother

Boys dressed as girls dancing

Coffins on bank, Bombret

Bombret

The Lowari Pass

Kalasha, old woman

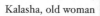

Kalasha, young woman

Farooq fishing

Panels restored by British Post
Office, Lahore

British Post Office, Lahore

Lahore Samina, Ghazala and Rehana

Javaid, guide, at Shalimar

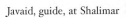

Chrysanthemums outside Avari Hotel

Lahore Fort, North Wall

Bats in Lawrence Gardens

15

History and Karachi

During much of my stay in Lahore, Farooq was absent. There were many people for him to renew friendship and acquaintance with. He enjoyed the company of groups of men, merely in the sense that he thrived in masculine company. When he did come home he appeared strangely Westernised in this Eastern setting. There were no strong voices until he returned. It seemed that living in the West had given him rough edges.

Rafique in contrast, had only visited England briefly, and was refined beyond most standards anywhere. His impeccable English repeatedly put mine to shame, and from time to time he sometimes visited with his wife. He remarked on one occasion that he had never seen an English person help around a Pakistani home in the way which I did. I think that it was at the time the dhobi had been absent for a few days and I was trying to help with the mountain of washing.

I also remember his comment about the British. He said that what he liked most about them was that they had left India at the time they did. I'm sure this observation carried great weight. Bearing in mind the blood bath prior to the foundation of Pakistan in 1947, and from what I read on the matter, Lord Wavell had been a good Viceroy and had devised a plan whereby, wherever a majority of Muslims predominated, that territory drawn out would form Pakistan. Tragically the plan was suddenly hurried towards the end by Mountbatten leading to much confusion and massive migrations of people. Muslims fleeing from India, Hindus fleeing to India. The Sikhs have remained a bone of contention in Pakistan, as they chose to side with the Hindu's in India. Stories of full trainloads of people being slaughtered as they crossed the border into Pakistan remain with Muslims. Finally, East and West Pakistan were formed to be one country. The idea of Pakistan is said to have come from Muhammad Iqbal, the revered Muslim poet. Mohammed Ali Jinnah, the Founder of Pakistan, is popularly known as Quaid-i-Azam (great leader).

Kashmir is even now a bone of contention for Pakistan, as of it holds a majority Muslim population but is 'occupied' by India according to the Pakistani viewpoint. Kashmir is significant for Pakistan because part of the Indus and its tributaries, which are the lifeblood of the country, have their source in that State.

When the Rafiques visited they normally sat in the first reception/ sitting room, the first on the left at the top of the stairs from the street. They were always treated with the greatest, respect with Lily and Rehana supplying tea and perhaps some small sweet dishes bought from nearby vendors. On one such visit, Rafique explained that he was required to travel to Karachi and would like Farooq, Lily and I to attend as his guests.

This was arranged and after a few days we all set off on the seven hundred and fifty mile or so first-class with air conditioning, top of the range of five classes, train journey. With Mr and Mrs Rafique, their daughter Farah, Lily, Farooq and myself restricted to a compartment, it seemed like a long trip. The stations along the route were a focal point of activity and always a welcome break to the tedium of travelling. It appeared possible to buy most types of food on the platforms. Vendors shouted, '*Samosa, samosa*', and some circulated with bunches of yellow bananas carried on their heads, some with spotted bananas. There are different names in Urdu for the different coloured bananas. Needless to say also curries, kebabs etc., could also be ordered—and supplied.

We stayed in a resthouse which Mr Rafique knew, and it was made pleasant by a constant breeze from the sea. Unfortunately, illness struck me again, this time in the form of, what they described as, a fever. All the available covers and mats were used in the resthouse to keep me warm, but running with perspiration, I still felt cold. I asked Farooq and Mr Rafique if they could get me a bottle of whisky.

This proved exceedingly difficult for them as alcohol generally is not approved of in Muslim Pakistan. After hours they returned with a small bottle which had cost the earth. It did help, even if it was only to alleviate the unpleasantness of the fever which lasted about 12 hours. My clothes were saturated, it was as if I had jumped into a swimming bath with them on, and it was almost possible to wring them out. But these type of fevers, it appeared, are an acceptable fact of Pakistani life and not at all to be concerned about, whatsoever. It was treated like an every day happening and it was apparent that I was making far too much fuss.

After my ordeal, we did manage to visit the Mausoleum of Quaid-i-Azam Mohammed Ali Jinnah, the founder of Pakistan. Later, at the harbour we watched boys diving for money which had been thrown into the water. I also watched mesmerised at an old wooden boat with improvised sail and a plank of wood sticking out from its side, on which boys crouched to give ballast, as it tacked, to and fro, around the harbour. It was searching to catch the right breeze direction in order to take it out to sea.

Further along from the harbour we found a mini-causeway and at the end, a fish shop. Although it sold hot battered fish that was the only similarity to ours. Seeped only in the hottest of spices, it had the effect of nearly blowing my head off. But after surviving the effect, one could not help remarking that it was very enjoyable!

On our return journey, Lily accompanied me in one of the third class type carriages, the rest of our group, probably wisely, kept to First. This was by my choice. I conveyed that I wished to see as much variety of life as possible whilst here. This potentially could have created a few ruffled feathers but there was no evidence of this.

We sat on latticed benches, much like garden seats and there was also a tier above where people reclined. It was busy and noisy and much of the carriage was taken up with piles of packages and bundles. But before departing from Karachi station, a long line of beggars in single file began weaving its way up from the platform and along the train corridor and aisles. Some used sticks as crutches, and some shuffled their bottoms along on small planks of wood, their legs were too thin and weak to support their body, this being the effect of rickets. These aides were as is seen in Brueghel paintings, rough hewn and rustic.

Some of the men in this procession were blind. Pakistan is a place where you can see a blind man leading another blind man and it happened on this occasion. There were so many maimed people, it was not possible to give each a rupee, which I normally tried to give, to individual beggars. All the corridors and passageways of the long train seemed to be taken up by this long, strangely silent stream of people with their overwhelmingly sad presence. This took about ten minutes to pass and after they had passed, their presence lingered.

The train eventually and thankfully, drew out from the station and although I can say by the time we arrived in Lahore, both Lily and I had sore bottoms due to our hard seats, the journey had been much more interesting than being closeted in cool air-conditioning. We had shared food with Sindhi people, and struck up conversations with other travellers and I felt generally we had a more colourful time. If Lily felt differently she certainly didn't show it.

Gladly back again in the apartment in Lahore, Dr Aftab said he too had had a fever during our absence. That night his eldest sister, the one who lived in another part of Lahore, visited. There was a long troubled conversation. I remember looking down from the flat roof to where they were talking in the yard below. The Doctor seemed uneasy and he happened to look up while I was looking down. Whatever the problem was, it was not disclosed.

16

Teas and the Village

Apart from sightseeing in Lahore, Farooq and I were expected, as visitors from England, to attend an interminable number of teas. I am not saying that this was any hardship! It was just at times there seemed to be an awful lot of them. Often we were merely asked to arrive before sundown. The invitations came from close and distant relatives, and friends of the family. Farooq, well aware a refusal could be deemed an insult, further explained it could engender ill feeling to accept some and not others, perhaps then jealousies would appear.

Lily or Rehana, or both, would accompany us, and with all the arranging and preparation of clothes, taxis to be phoned for from next door, or rickshaws or tongas to be found out on the streets, teas took up a large part of our lives. Two of the redeeming factors of the teas were the delicious *samosas* and the fruit *chaat*, both important elements in the Pakistani tea. At a cousin's mother's these home made treats were markedly delicious, and although it is considered well mannered to show appreciation by eating plenty, I think that here I managed to exceed the acceptable bounds. I ate so much that afterwards I went to sleep on their settee.

The offence cannot have been too great, as after I awoke the host's son, Jaleel, Farooq's cousin, invited us to visit him at his house, and asked what my interests were. He seemed intent on catering for some sporting pursuit I might have. Not athletic whatsoever, I mentioned that I did have a horse about eight years before and used to like horse-riding. Hardly had the words passed my lips than he said that he would arrange it.

A couple of days later, on arriving in our white van after a two hour drive, Jaleel's wife and children greeted us. He had arranged everything regarding the horse-riding, and we were to be in a Mr Choudri's hands, a very respected land owner, who lived in a small village close to Choukleborough where we now were.

After a discussion concerning a five year irrigation plan for Pakistan of which Jaleel was very proud, because he was one of the people implementing it, and it was developing extremely well, accompanied by chai, curry and chapati, we trundled off in our van to a village where the riding exercise was being arranged.

Nestled about a hundred and fifty yards from the dusty single-file road along the canal bank was Mr Choudri's stone built house. The fact that it was stone had particular significance because all other accommodation in the village consisted of badly built brick buildings which were partially mud-covered. After the customary salutations, Farooq was invited to stay with Mr Choudri and I was relegated to what I can only describe as the farmyard. I was told no women ever stayed in the stone house, so that meant that I was joining all the females in the Choudri family.

This, as it turned out, was superlatively more interesting than mere creature comforts. Apart from a small room for sleeping and a small utility area, a small hut with a dry toilet, cooking pots, beds haphazardly placed and an abundance of hens scratching about in all this: there was nothing much else apparent. At the far end toward the lane a man was trudging about with a stave, mixing two or three types of mud together in order to cover the brick walls.

Mr Choudri's mother was proudly introduced to me, I was told that she was so old, that no one in fact knew exactly how old. She was the first I met of a particular breed of woman in Pakistan whom previously I had no idea existed. She was above following the traditions expected of women in a Muslim country and was strongly hooked on tobacco. If she wasn't sitting on the side of a bed inhaling from a large hookah, a manservant who was treated with disdain and as a fool, was busy preparing it for her. He, by the way, must previously have had his nose broken, as it appeared crooked and nearer to one side of his face than the other.

Other Pakistani etiquette also appeared to have been abandoned in the yard. For example generally speaking it is not accepted as being desirable that women chew betel nuts. It is said that betel nuts, eaten with aniseed and other spices and wrapped in a leaf become habitual if taken early in life. Some ingredient in this sweet dyes the mouth and teeth dark red. This made it easy to spot those who were partial, and there was plenty of evidence here!

Young Mrs Choudri, the wife of the landlord, an upright, large, middle aged woman busied herself cooking with aluminium pots over small stick fires in a corner of the yard. Her three tall sons came to observe from time to time. When standing alongside each other, their heights appeared to step down in equal tiers, as if their age gaps had been perfectly arranged. I could not help wondering where the Choudri offspring had been conceived. That is, if women did not stay in the stone house.

Much later in the afternoon, as if to add insult to injury, the old Mrs Choudri stripped off her kamiz in front of all. This was a fair sight as she was not wearing anything underneath, someone just calmly handed her a clean one. Female nakedness in public being taboo in Pakistan I was somewhat surprised by this exhibition, but no one batted an eyelid.

Shortly after, Farooq came to tell me that at last the horses were ready. He took me to a small steel grey pony tethered to a tree, somewhere between the perimeter of the mud village and the stone house. Close by a young man was having difficulty holding on to the reins of a young flighty, dark brown mare who stood at about 15.2 hands high.

In cowardly fashion I thought it may be wiser to ride the pony and attempt to weigh up the situation. Women, children, men, young and old, were congregating on the strip of land between the canal and the village. I mounted the grey pony, which was rather small for me, and was very awkward and stubborn. It persisted in going around in very small circles and there was not a great deal that I could do about it. Feeling extremely foolish and rather embarrassed, because there were so many people watching, and not wishing to disappoint them, I had no option but to ride the prancing brown mare, or at least try.

When I was successfully, with help, seated in the red saddle, with high pommel and straps for stirrups, only then did I realise what a beautiful creature this was. Walking quietly around the crowd, and then venturing a controlled trot, I was very aware that she was keen to be off. This was why I tried to do everything as quietly and calmly as possible. Having circled the crowd of people a couple of times I came across Farooq who said;

'Why don't you ride her?'

Whether my nerves were still frayed by our journey especially his driving in Turkey or what, I don't know, but I was a little rattled by the question.

'What does he think I am doing?' I muttered to myself and momentarily forgot what kind of horse I was riding and pressed my heels into the mare's sides.

She seemed to leap out into the failing light, twilight was upon us and it doesn't last long in this part of the world. Feeling the mare's strength I glanced over my shoulder saying to Farooq,

'I can't stop her!' She could travel, and she went at speed. The problem was that if I just sat there and let her run herself out, and if I didn't fall off, I wouldn't know where I would end up. And as I didn't know the name of the village I had just left, nor spoke the language, how could I ask directions to find my way back?

There was another consideration and that was I didn't want her to break a leg so I decided to put my energy into stopping her, even if I had to use foul methods. I resorted to sawing the mare's mouth with her bit. This is something I had never previously done and thankfully never since. But it did not have much effect. The wind made her mane flow and she liked it.

Coming up ahead were irrigation ditches. I had heard about tubewells and did not know quite what they were or whether they could harm her or both of us. Sitting well into the saddle and praying prior to the first ditch, she lifted from the ground like a bird.

What a magnificent creature she was! She further impressed me by going over a couple more. At the next one, by taking her at a slight angle over the hurdle I managed at last to break her gait and then by facing her into a thorn bush, eventually I stopped her. Neither of us were even scratched.

Quietly dismounting and talking softly, I walked beside her as much to calm myself as well as her. Retracing our steps I knew I would need to get on again otherwise my nerve would be lost. With trepidation, I remounted and continued our sedate walk. We were then met by Farooq coming to look for us and talking avidly to a group of young men from the village.

'Why were you frightened?' He asked, seemingly my remark about not being able to stop her had sparked this question. I had thought that I had assessed the situation and acted accordingly, so again his question ruffled me and when answering, my voice, I think, rose ever so slightly. Affected by this, the mare's ears pricked forward again and off she was once more, this time toward the still waiting villagers.

I laid back toward her rump to get more leverage on the reins, as we circled around the group to cheers and clapping. Making a spectacle of myself had been far from my intention. Greatly embarrassed, we headed back once more to the brick buildings in the village and this time there was a little stream which slowed her down and making use of a wall as a barrier, she came to an abrupt stop.

Both of us by now were rather tired, we made our way quietly back to the tree where the grey pony had been tethered. I dismounted, the front of my ankle bled from my foot slipping too far into the leather thong stirrup. To my great surprise, Mr Choudri was there to greet me and shook my hand warmly with congratulations! My legs were still quaking when he said that he would be honoured if I would stay in his stone built house that night!

Farooq slept nearby and I left my bedroom door open to cool the room and also left the fan on. Being well rested by morning, I was only to meet with insistence from all around that I should ride the mare again. The local school was to be closed—I suppose it was anticipated that there would be a repeat performance. When I at last saw the mare again she looked toward me as if there was love in her eyes, but I was determined not to be fooled again, and rigged up a martingale to have more control of her flighty head.

Quietly at a gentle canter we passed the children who cheered excitedly, and trotting about a mile up the canal bank road we thankfully returned without incident. Farooq told me later that while he and Mr Choudri were having breakfast, people would enter and report exactly where we were.

On returning eventually to the yard alone, Mr Choudri's wife was very insistent that I should eat. I felt dreadfully sick, which she interpreted, I guess, as an insult to her cooking, and frustrated by this she took it upon herself to spoon-feed me. To add further incongruity to the situation, a couple arrived from Lyallpur, a fashionable town I was told, and sitting on the beds we discussed politics. Barely an inch of flesh was visible on one arm of the young woman as it was covered in gold bracelets. Over her shoulder I could still see the man still trudging around mixing the different kinds of mud.

On the road back to Lahore, Farooq explained that Mr Choudri had not approved of my riding techniques. I should not have tried to stop the horse in the way that I did, also I should have rubbed her down, and I was absolutely in agreement. Farooq had also learned that no one had ever dared to gallop the horse full tilt before. They were scared to.

17

Eastern Life, Loose Ends and Shalimar

Home again in the apartment I realised nearly four weeks had elapsed and it was time at least to think about departure. I was saddened by the thought that this blissful time must end, this was not going to be an easy task emotionally. Nothing had been too difficult for this family in accommodating me. Never was there a complaint or a face pulled at a request or a desire. Some of my western tastes must have been awkward but I was not made aware of them being such, nor did I feel out of place. I remember now with great love, the hospitality given and the effect this had on my life at the time. It restored a belief that perhaps human beings are not all bad, a belief in the human aspect of Mankind as being positive.

Westerners are in the privileged position of being able to help the developing world, but personally I learned a great deal about what I believe are important values from the people I met in the East. I learned a little about compassion, caring and the love which binds families together. I also learned about humility. In the East there are sayings which mean it is superior to serve than to be served. I still feel humbled by the way I was treated. The experience also awakened respect for how these people conducted their lives. Not just this family but many living in the most abject and crowded conditions, but managing to retain civility, dignity, and respect towards companions and others.

All this may sound idealistic to Westerners. There is, of course, the other side, no peoples are ever perfect. There are criminals, like elsewhere, and class distinction is rife. There is exploitation, corruption and accompanying negative destructive elements. I have merely been talking about the people I met and what I observed.

To disentangle myself from life in Lahore, especially when I was so happy and the will to do so had become muted, took great effort. It meant attending the government building each day to attempt to have my passport stamped. The problem was the van. It was officially owned by me, and there were very strict rules about foreigners leaving vehicles behind. I pleaded that because of illness it was necessary to travel back by plane, and this was not totally untrue. Farooq would later return in the van. This was eventually written in my passport and also Farooq's. But this then needed to be stamped in another department. Each day we went, the clerk could not quite bring himself to do it

While not at the government building there were loose ends to resolve before departure, and I was intent on enjoying the valuable remaining time. A visit to the famous Shalimar Gardens could not be postponed further.

On Sunday morning Farooq, Mr Rafique, his daughter and I strolled around the terraces of the gardens on pathways of tiles designed in different patterns. The levels of the three terraces were connected by ramps. Laid out in the reign of the great Shah Jahan in the 1640s, these gardens had been designed for the Emperor to view on horseback. It took little imagination, especially after viewing Mughal miniatures, to visualize a group of ornately decorated Arab horses and an even more ornately dressed Emperor and his entourage. Each would be astride a horse with its nostrils dilated, prancing along the paths and ramps.

On one terrace was a pond with two pagodas. It had been designed to manifest reflection at certain times of day. At night it would have been lit by hundreds of candles and no doubt the reflection of the moon would have been considered. There was a scalloped skirting around the water's edge, when looked at together with its reflection, dark circles within the surrounding white of the skirting could be seen. Symmetry was everywhere, even in the placing of the ornate urns full of vivid coloured blooms. But how nice it would have been to have seen an Emperor on horse-back mirror-imaged on the blue water!

Another issue to resolve, was the visit to Lily and Rehana's friend, Aftab's prospective wife. After tea at her house I was asked to look at her needlework and embroidery, almost like a judge at a Cumbrian Agriculture show. I didn't look at it with regard to the competence which was blatantly apparent, but rather as an indication of expression of the individual. Rather like looking at someone's painting.

This whole experience placed me in a difficult position. I was probably not objective, certainly I saw the Doctor in a very different light to how his sisters viewed him. I saw areas in his character, rightly or wrongly, which I did not feel that his potential wife could be sensitive to. If I was dishonest when giving my judgement perhaps I would be partly responsible for him not being happily married, if that indeed was to be the case. In the end I just told him what I thought. Although I suppose

I envied the girl I hope any judgement made was not impaired by jealousy. Perhaps also what I said did not hold much weight anyway as his two sisters now seemed very decided about the marriage.

Prior to all this, one evening after our visit to Nankana, Aftab and I had had a most peculiar if not poetic exchange. He had said,

'I liked a girl in the country and I liked a girl in the town. But if I had to choose, I would choose the girl in the town. I think I tried to ascertain whether there were two girls or just one and failing this I asked him if she was tall. He replied,

'She is tall and her back is very straight.'

'Is she taller than you?' I had asked. He chuckled, 'Oh no,' he said, 'I could never like a woman taller than myself!'

The visit to his future wife had been a sobering experience and so with visiting the government office. By this time the passports had been stamped, but now Farooq and I were visiting another room in the building for an official to initial the stamp. The same thing was happening, he could not quite do this and there were the tears in his eyes just like the custom's officer earlier who would not let us into Pakistan. It hadn't been easy to get into this country and now it wasn't easy to get out!

My flight was booked for three days' time, almost five weeks had elapsed, as nonchalantly as any five weeks could ever pass. A mango party had been arranged for the children, this was quite a common event and different families acted as hosts. It was similar to our children's birthday parties.

Neighbour's children thronged into two of the rooms of the apartment, as well as the six children from Farooq's family. They being Bilal, Ghazala, Samina, Ahmed, Ghazali and baby Anse who attended in Rehana's arms. Mangoes chilled between chunks of ice in buckets were brought in. Lily and I helped in cutting segments of mango flesh from the large stones. It was possible to score the flesh with a knife and give the mango whole to the eater. They then merely extracted a wedge and sucked the fruit away from the skin. These parties often turned into competitions and some children boasted of the number of mangoes consumed at such and such a party.

Mr and Mrs Rafique treated me to a further visit to Anarkali Bazaar where we looked at brass plates with inlaid copper designs and Mrs R said that she would like me to choose some fabric which she would have embroidered in the form that I wished. Lily also took me on an outing to a fabric shop on the Mall, one of the more wealthy streets in Lahore.

She insisted that I should choose a shawl. I tried to resist, but it was Aftab's gift and he had seemingly given her specific instructions. She eventually wangled me into choosing a Kashmiri hand-woven shawl with embroidered motifs so beautifully stitched it was almost impossible to differentiate the front from the back. We returned from the shop by bus and my head swam a little thinking perhaps the Doctor really liked me a little after all.

My passport was now in order and I was to leave the following day. Aftab had given the money for my air ticket and that final night had invited a group of dancers to entertain us. The dancing children were, in fact, boys dressed as girls.

18

The Parting

In the morning neighbours and family friends congregated to wish me well. Even more gifts arrived such as ornate slippers from a friend of Farooq's, the one who was to accompany him on his return journey in the van. In all this melange little Ghazali put himself into a large cardboard box and said that he would like to come too!

'Soni Auntie, Soni Auntie!' That is what he called me, Soni meaning pretty. I certainly did not want to leave him, but nor could I take him with me—on this occasion, at least. His father and I had said our goodbyes the night before. He had actually allowed me to photograph him with his children. This was a compliment, as normally he felt picture taking was not being quite true to the keeping of his faith. I also photographed him with Ghazali alone, but sadly, and rather strangely, my camera with the film still inside, disappeared from the Royal Academy when I returned. It is with regret that I think of this now and also recalling what follows.

Although it may have seemed joyful to any imaginary observers of the scene of parting, I am still able to feel that deep feeling of being torn away from something very dear, also of dread and apprehension of travelling such a long distance on my own.

Garlands of fresh blossom mounted around my neck from well wishers. This is usually a custom for the bride and groom in wedding ceremonies! Honoured I was, and alongside the peach and pink blooms, a string of tinsel with a sequined silver heart completed the adornment.

Farooq, Aftab, Rehana, Lily and the Rafiques accompanied me to the airport. As we stood in the reception area, Aftab told me that the suit that I was wearing, the one which I had especially made in Kabul, was the same as that of a Socialialist-minded leader. It was in the exact same style and colour. He went on to say:

'The poor man was shot a few months ago.'

'Oh,' I gasped, 'Why?'

'Because he had led a hundred workers, and for doing so, had been shot down dead.' Armed with this snippet of information and making me feel a little uneasy, the moment I was dreading most had come. It was time to say goodbye.

With heavy heart, as they all stood smiling in their little group, I wished each of them well, especially Farooq for his return journey. I shook hands with all the men and embraced each of the women. Rehana and I held each other for a long time. Tearing myself away, garlanded, my insides feeling as heavy as lead, I boarded the plane. Aftab, knowing my dislike for excesses, had given me six toffees for the ascents and descents, thinking the plane's flight would only be broken at Karachi and Moscow. There were only sufficient for this.

Once I was seated in the plane the faces of the family kept appearing and fading in my mind's eye, almost like a sea in the form of a pyramid or Hindu temple. Aftab's face twinkled from everywhere, I was so distracted that I absent-mindedly ate some of a bouquet of flowers which had also been given. Seated to my left was a young Pakistani girl leaving her home for the first time. We both wept when the wheels left the ground and we ascended into the ultramarine sky.

On being greeted in Karachi by airport porters I was asked, because of my garlands, if I had come from the Bahamas! I spent a very lonely night in a hotel named Hostelerie Francais which had nothing to do with anything I knew about France. I missed the warm company of Farooq's family. This was the first time I had been alone for a considerable number of months. In the morning, whilst breakfasting on boiled egg, I was interrupted on two occasions by men from the airport asking if I had had a good night and was I enjoying my breakfast!

This time on the plane I sat between a Kashmiri gentleman and the same Pakistani girl. It was now for real, we were leaving Pakistani soil for the final time. Needless to say, the girl and I really wept when we left Pakistani ground.

Over the Arabian Ocean, diffuse pastel hues and shades of great depth and luminosity enveloped the plane. We flew on, over lines and lines of rock formations resembling small tiers on the edges of a ginger cake mix, across mile on mile of desert, seeing, just once, a long road punctuated by a roundabout and the long straight road continuing.

As we descended, circling Moscow in grey light, I asked the Kashmiri why the houses and skyscrapers were built the way in which they were. Isolated little streets of terraced cottages looked depressed and repressed as if they had been taken from the centre of old Salford, and been

plonked down in an almost rural setting. It was the large spaces around
the lonely streets and between the tawdry multi-floored skyscraper flats
that appeared strange. The Kashmiri replied:

'It would be difficult to bomb them with conventional weapons.'

Around the airport ample women in pairs, belted in heavy tweed coats,
pushed trucks, which would have taken four men in our country. This was
a far cry from the feminine chiffoned women of Pakistan, I couldn't help
thinking.

When we left the plane the cold made our teeth chatter. And as we
entered a visitors checkpoint a tall uniformed armed guard took our
passports. After negotiating an extremely tall metal-barred revolving
turnstile I found myself in a large hall. Looking for a canteen, I was
distracted by embroidered haberdasheries in a glass case. I thought these
items too, looked equally cold, although the stitch work was finely
done.

Then I found that somehow I had became dissociated from the other
passengers. After attempting, in vain, to find somewhere I could buy a
coffee and feeling somewhat warmer from anxiety, I felt it prudent to
retrace my steps. This too did not prove easy either. Being left here would
be no joke, in a place seemingly designed to confuse passengers by its
complication of split levels!

I later heard that a young girl, a friend of a Persian friend of mine had
also become lost and finished up in hysterical tears in this very place.
Fortunately for me, however, it was with some measured relief that I
found the guard by the turnstile again. I was still feeling uneasy as I was
alone with an armed man who totally ignored me for what seemed like a
long time. I was also still without my passport, plus the cold again caught
up with me.

Slowly the passengers started to return in dribs and drabs, after they
had had coffee in the restaurant, I never did ascertain its whereabouts.
Braced, and in line, we each negotiated the horrendous turnstile and
thankfully all our passports were returned and no one was detained!

After our unanticipated touchdown in Frankfurt, when I finished my
last toffee, it was not long before I was saying goodbye to the Kashmiri
gentleman in the pale grey drizzle outside the London Cromwell Road
Terminus. I had intended to merely head for my flat on the Uxbridge
Road and sleep for a few days. With the five hours difference between
Pakistani time and ours it was about thirty hours previously that I had
said final goodbyes to my friends in Lahore.

I was glad to be back at my London flat, but before resting I thought I should ring my parents to let them know. Misguided, by my mother's pleading to come home, and although suffering from profound jet lag even whilst ringing her, later that night, I foolishly caught the train to Carlisle. My mother had insisted that I should get a sleeper, which she would pay for, and if I was still asleep at Carlisle she would wake me!

Needless to say I didn't manage to find the time to ask the guard for a sleeping compartment, I was asleep before that. I overshot Carlisle and finished up in Kilmarnock. Seemingly, I later learnt, my mother and one or two of my sisters had invaded all the sleeping compartments on the train at Carlisle although some of the occupants were only partly dressed!

On the Kilmarnock platform I was unaware of the shenanigans at Carlisle. There was an hour long wait for the Glasgow train to take me back. I was though very aware of the morning wind, like a whip on my cheeks, and it reminded me cruelly that I was a great distance from Ghazali and Pakistan. But one thing I knew that I had learnt from my sweet sojourn, was the meaning of the words in Robert Burn's song, 'My Love is like a Red, Red Rose': which may well have been written, quite close to where I was standing!

Part Three

Part Three

19

Afterthoughts and Further Journeying

Farooq arrived back in London with his friend, Saleem, about six months after me. Unfortunately, the old van had an accident in Bulgaria, where it remained. Farooq carried the table Aftab had given me on his back, changing trains all the way from Sofiya back to London.

I had thought Farooq may settle down after visiting his homeland; that was one of the reasons I made the journey with him. The trip, sadly, had the opposite effect and Farooq became even more unsettled. He started travelling back and forth between England and Pakistan.

I am not saying that I regret for one moment the journey overland to Pakistan, especially crossing the desert in Iran which made me view the world very differently. It gave me a view with perspective both regarding distances and problems. I became, for the first time, very aware that England is a very small country. After the journey, the kind of problems here appeared comparatively like a storm in a tea cup. Also, many of the difficulties here, as contained in a tea cup, seemed to be refracted. In other words, dealing with the same problem recurring many times and merely from different angles. In Iran, lack of water, stable government, education, basic medical assistance, although perhaps much simpler to identify, are infinitely more grave and difficult to solve.

In the summer of 1973 I visited Farooq whilst he was staying with his family in Lahore. From our correspondence he was especially looking forward to my visit. This time I travelled with Air Alia. Pakistani time being five hours ahead of ours meant there were a succession of meals, as they were served in accordance with local time. There were, therefore, two breakfasts and two lunches.

It was not long after coming back to Lahore, that I began to find the late July heat, the dust and the feeling of oppression of city life almost unbearable. Like the British during the Raj, I felt the lure of the mountains in the North and the cooler air.

Farooq and I changed our minds many times. Would it be the beautiful Kaghan Valley, or the Vale of Swat where Asoka reigned in 273–232 BC and a Graeco-Buddhist civilization had flourished? Or perhaps Chitral, part of which is inhabited by the Kalash Tribes, said to be descended from peoples left behind on the grand march of Alexander the Great?

After more discussion and advice from Dr Aftab and Zulfiqar, we opted for the latter. We set off in a crowded white Transit van and sped across the Punjabi plain, crossing the Chenab and Jhelum, tributaries of the Indus. The word Punjab means, in fact, five rivers, the other three tributaries being the Ravi, on which Lahore stands, the Sutlej and the Beas. We saw fields and fields of people calf deep in water plodding in mud planting small rice plants.

In Peshawar we were well rested after one night in a hotel, before setting off on the 191 mile journey. We were able to take the bus to Dir. From there only four-wheel drive jeep travel was possible. We stopped by a gushing, grey river, travelling at great speed from the Hindukush. I just wouldn't have dared cross the flimsy footbridge spanning the torrent. We had read from typed sheets of paper issued by the Tourist Office in Lahore that there was local wine available. A man crossed the flimsy bridge in search of a bottle, I hardly dared to look. He returned brandishing one above his head.

We climbed for some time up the Lowari Pass of 10,230 feet. We rose above the morning mists, it reminded me of Chinese paintings. The white mist swirled encircling the bases of mountains and trees, only leaving their tips visible. I had always thought Chinese paintings were impossible until then. We entered into a concealed world above the delicate cloud.

After the Pass, we looked back at the road which seemed a zigzagging ribbon almost impossible to traverse. We passed a lorry which had left the road and was halfway down a ravine. Men were pulling on ropes trying to put it back on its wheels. Streams gushed down from the mountains and crossed our road then continued their descent. Often the road needed to be rebuilt due to the constant onslaught of water.

When we arrived in the small market town of Chitral, we looked for somewhere to stay. We asked other visitors if they could recommend anywhere, but most said there were bugs in the hotels and resthouses. We were unsure about what to do. Our experience of bugs in Iran was uppermost in our minds.

When we were coming away from the bazaar, a gentleman in a jeep disembarked and came towards us. He was a very dignified version of James Coburn and walked with a stick. This wonderfully refined gentleman, as it turned out was the Prince of Chitral no less! The then President, Zulfiqar Ali Bhutto, Benazir's father, had stripped all titled people of their titles. Despite this most people still referred to this gentleman as the Prince. Bhutto was also responsible for the idea that tenants of land should become owners. This had resulted in land owners arming themselves for their own safety.

The Prince asked us what was our problem. We explained our reluctance in staying in any of the hotels. He told us that he was having a hotel built near to his palace and it was called Tirich Mir View. It had not quite been completed, and there were no staff at present, but we would be welcome to stay.

Farooq and I were quite overwhelmed by this gratuitous offer and said we would be delighted. We were told we would be its first visitors.

As very honoured guests we moved in, overlooking the magnificent spectacle of Tirich Mir, 25,263 feet, which straddled the head the valley. Having said there were no servants, the Prince then sent us a kindly fellow to cook for us anything we wished. Or more accurately, what was available. Local produce was mainly limited to chicken, vegetables, rice and flour. Despite this, it was all delicious and we couldn't believe our good fortune, the whole of the ground floor to ourselves, which was spacious, and a servant. The mountain almost smiled down on us!

20

Bombret and Garam Chashma

The Kalash tribes mainly lived in three valleys, Brior, Rumber and Bombret. We decided to visit Bombret as it was said to be the most picturesque. We hired a guide, and were able to use a jeep to just beyond Ayun. From there it was apparent that the road was unfit, so we were obliged to walk the remaining eight miles.

We followed a stream up to a few wooden huts on its banks. Close by we had passed some rough hewn coffins set back from the path and shaded by trees. The custom was to leave the dead above ground.

We were invited into one of the huts for tea. The women were very proud in showing us their headdresses. One of these was a strip of heavy black felt about eight inches wide. It was decorated with rows and rows of numerous shells, old buttons and any other objects considered attractive; the summer headdresses were much lighter in weight.

I wondered, because I was so fascinated with the black headdress, if I could perhaps purchase it. The owner was quite willing, but she said she would have to ask her husband who was working on the wooded slopes nearby.

When she returned it was apparent her husband had been extremely annoyed. She had been told she must not part with the headdress. This is not surprising as our guide told us that the Kalasha women often wore the same clothes most of their lives. Bits would be added and stitched into the garment when necessary. Only in death, when there was great celebration and people came from surrounding valleys, the corpse would be fitted with new clothes.

Other than funerals, another great celebration these tribes had were marriages. The bride is said to be purified by smoke from a fire then a goat is killed, and its head passed through the flames. Tradition and heredity play a major part in Kalasha life. A person who converts to Islam is no longer considered Kalasha.

Other information gleaned was that women ground pigment for their facial makeup. Also, that partly due to being marginalised and suffering poverty, Goitre was prevalent in 60-80 per cent of children due to iodine deficiency.

We made another visit, using the hotel as a base, to Garam Chashma, meaning hot springs. The place is very well known throughout Pakistan, and noted for the medicinal quality of the water. Adjoined to our comfortable resthouse was a room containing a concrete bath which was about six foot square. It was extremely pleasant immersing oneself in the beautiful warm water.

In the evening I decided to sample some of the wine we had previously acquired. To my great surprise it had the effect of removing the top off my head. I'm sure it must have been close to pure alcohol!

During our stay we befriended a young boy called Wakeel. He was perhaps 12 years old and passionately wanted to learn to read and write. His schooling had been spasmodic, in fact, almost non-existent. Farooq gave him simple exercises and I helped him with his English.

In the daytime we watched Wakeel fish. The rainbow trout were like fast fleeting shadows darting under stones in the fast, fresh, crystal water. In order to catch them, Wakeel illustrated, you needed to be faster and cleverer than they. He landed three or four in a very short space of time. Farooq and I spent the rest of the day selecting possible likely places to fish, but our efforts of trying to fish like Wakeel were not rewarded. We returned with nothing.

There was an atmosphere of great ease in the village, no pressures. People pursued various occupations such as washing clothes, roasting walnuts, or eating them, or collecting mulberries which grew lavishly on the many trees around.

Behind our resthouse and further up the hill were a number of wooden dilapidated buildings which held larger tanks of warm spring water, I enjoyed swimming in one of these. Farooq declined, preferring to talk to the local people.

Before we left the following day, Farooq gave his best white T-shirt to a man in the village who needed one. I always believed that Farooq would give the shirt off his back! Not content with this, he directed that I give Wakeel a brown suit I had just bought in Gulberg, a fashionable part of Lahore. I relented eventually, and Wakeel gave me two extra large, roughly cut garnets.

There were lots of these stones and some lapis lazuli in and around Chitral. People said the Afghan travellers brought them into the area to barter for food. The Chitralis then sell them to tourists.

Also in the bazaar in Chitral you could find lots of what looked like second hand clothes shops. Heavy tweed coats in old fashioned western styles were said to come from charities in the Communist bloc.

Back in the hotel, the Prince and his family visited. I say his family, they were numerous, and all women and children. To the west of Tirich Mir, on the top of one of the mountains, was another of the Prince's palaces. I couldn't imagine how he and his family could actually access this dwelling, because of the steepness, remoteness, and height.

In order to see the Prince play polo we stayed a few days longer than originally intended, however, just before the match was due on the Saturday, it was cancelled. This was in commiseration for all the people who had lost their lives, or suffered in the heavy flooding further south.

21

The Journey Back

After re-negotiating the Lowari Pass of over 10,000 feet by jeep, this time from the opposite direction, our difficulties began. Monsoon rain started at Dir, where we stayed the night. We rose at an unearthly hour to catch the government coach back to Peshawar.

The rain was like a continuous sheet of water. On our way to the bus terminus a man shot out of an alleyway and grabbed me, so hard that he left my arms tingling with pain. He disappeared as quickly as he had appeared, back into the sheet of water.

There was a delay at the terminus, and much chatter as to whether the journey would be possible. An hour late, we started off in the unpainted, silver coloured, metal coach.

At the first torrent which came down the mountainside and crossed the road, before continuing its descent, we stopped. The water appeared wild in its speed as it crossed over the road. The driver disembarked and began to ford the stream by foot, poking with a stick, just to check whether the bus could make it across.

We managed this crossing and another four, the driver testing each one, prior to the bus. On the sixth a mishap occurred. About halfway across, the back end of the coach caught on a large boulder. The driver revved and revved. Then shouted for all to disembark, except me. I think this was because I was the only female. Most of the passengers started pushing from the back. With the loud noise of the engine, and glancing out of the window at the bottomless drop, feeling the situation to be precarious, I too left the bus.

The more the driver revved, the more the panels were being ripped off from the back of the coach. Many people suggested remedies including Farooq. He said if the road was dug away at the front of the bus, the problem would be relieved. An argument ensued. Hoping to give time for the problem to be resolved, we decided to make our way to a cafe up the road.

Out of dirty cups without handles we sipped our *chai*. It was still comforting as we sat and watched the relentless rain outside. We strolled slowly back with a number of other people. One was an American traveller who had walked over the Shandur Pass from Gilgit and had been walking for weeks. I was in awe of the magnitude of his walk, the Shandur being over 12,000 feet. The Lowari from Dir and the Shandur from Gilgit are the only two passes into Chitral. These routes are only open from June to early September, they are snowbound for the rest of the year.

The American kept making notes, perhaps for a book. When we returned, the situation had still not been resolved, in fact it was compounded. A line of vehicles had collected behind the bus, so many, we couldn't see its end, as it wound around two bends into the distance. There were lorries carrying sleepers, wagons, jeeps, all pipping their horns! Some people were using sleepers off the lorries to try to jack up the back end of the bus.

Some men pushed from the front then went to the back and pushed. Voices were raised and there was some confusion. Then it happened, some pushed from the front at the same time as those pushing from the back. In my mind's eye I saw the bus concertina up the hillside!

Eventually, the road builders arrived and managed to relieve the bus of the troublesome boulder. Seated thankfully back in the bus, the atmosphere was more friendly than before, most people joked and became deep in conversation. The boulder must have brought us closer together.

Hours later we arrived at a town on a plain surrounded by acres and acres of sweet corn. The driver found there was no diesel because of the difficulty of transporting it during the flooding. He placed his head in his hands and was near to bursting into tears.

Farooq and I left the American and his friend in order to find something to eat. Roasted sweet corn, not surprisingly, was the only thing we could find. There was a three-hour wait for the diesel.

We arrived at our destination, Peshawar, at 1.00 a.m. The journey on the government coach had taken around nineteen hours. It was all too much for the driver, who must have been close to exhaustion. This time he did break down and weep. The passengers each shook his hand and congratulated him.

On our way to Lahore we found bridges washed away and a devastated countryside. The small rice plants which had been lovingly planted, were now strewn everywhere, alongside railway sleepers and uprooted trees.

We stopped for four hours at a Bailey bridge as the traffic could only cross in single file one way, and only very slowly. People entered our Ford Transit and told tales of lost ones. One man described how he had raised a child on his shoulders with water rising to his chin. Everyone was angry. They said bodies had floated down the river, and had come from India, and they had had no warning of this catastrophe. The irrigation system in Pakistan had recently been changed aiming to retain even more water, and had added to the severity of the flooding.

We managed after this to reach Lahore without any further problems. The Ravi Bridge, thankfully, was intact. I noticed nomadic settlements which had been present prior to our journey were not there now. Whether the people had left or their camps had been washed away, I don't know.

The family back home had been worried about us. Lily and Rehana were glad to see us. My parents had sent a telegram days ago asking me to let them know I was OK, which I did immediately. Farooq and I had been blissfully ignorant of the severity of the floods prior to the few days before leaving Chitral.

22

Nankana and Goodbye

Before making the journey into the mountains we had visited Nankana Sahib, Aftab's home, and discussed with him which of the valleys to visit whether it should be Swat, Kaghan or Chitral. After the trip we were to visit the Doctor again, he had arranged another riding exercise for me.

Farooq and I travelled to a canal quite close to Nankana but different to, where the first riding escapade took place. We were well into the heart of the countryside and a long way from villages or dwellings. A small group of men had congregated and stood by a wonderful white stallion, no less. It seemed very fit and a little frisky. They told me it was a dancing horse. I didn't wish to let Aftab down or the people who had arranged this, so although fearful, mounted the animal. A little gingerly we followed the canal bank away from the group and eventually risked a trot.

It was soon apparent that the horse didn't respond to the usual riding commands. Such as stopping when you pulled the reins. Fortunately, after what seemed like a long time, and well away from the group, we came to a fence. This horse thankfully did not attempt to jump it, and I managed to turn around, back in the direction of the men and Farooq.

The group were now stood on a small bridge, close to them, the horse decided to wade into the water, up to its belly. I had little control of where it decided to go and felt its legs starting to give way, like a horse does before it rolls. He obviously wanted to cool himself, with me on its back! Nervously, I gave some very short, sharp jerks on the reins and closely avoided a minor catastrophe in the nick of time! The men seemed mildly amused, I wasn't.

When I did dismount I asked how they normally stopped the horse. They explained because it was a special horse for dancing, usually at weddings and funerals, it had a totally different set of commands. For instance to stop it you patted its neck. How could I have guessed? I said it would have been helpful if they had told me this before I attempted the ride.

Later that day, saying goodbye to the Doctor in the road outside his surgery, his hand arrived in slow motion before shaking mine. As if to again, prolong the sad moment. It has to be said he was now married to Shama, meaning the light of the candle. He had told me they would have light all the time: his sunlight during the day and hers during the night. Now they had spiritual light as well, because their first child's name was Noor.

23

Intermittent Communication and 1975

Farooq visited Cumbria two or three times between 1973 and 75. I visited Poole, Dorset where he was working, once. Now it felt like each time we parted our relationship was severed a little bit more. But we did write and in 1975 he wanted me to visit him again in Pakistan. He had produced a Pakistani feature film 'Sajjan Kamla' meaning the lovesick fool.

We met at Karachi Airport. Farooq had business regarding his film so we planned to stay a few days in a friend's flat. I had imagined a visit to the film distributors to be a rather salubrious affair and dressed accordingly.

Faisal, the co-producer, Farooq and I arrived by taxi, the windows of which would not go up, hence my hair, which I had taken trouble with, was now a mass of tangles. A large billboard covered the front of the building. We ascended by some dirty wooden littered stairs, some of the wall between this, and the next door dwelling had been demolished. Families peered at us as we ascended. Perhaps they hoped to see famous film stars.

The office was equally unglamorous and Faisal and Farooq had an uphill struggle arriving at any deal. It was pointed out that they should have visited prior to the film's release in Lahore, where it had been given a B rating. It was all very disappointing for Farooq and his friend.

We then searched for someone in another part of town who owed them money. After that, we headed for the sea at Clifton. We arrived as the sun was setting behind three small islands. Men hung about with fine prancing horses and the beach was a sea of mud, churned by camels plodding up and down giving rides. Along the coast was a wrecked, rusted tanker. A little inland was the silhouette of a Sikh temple and another dome nearby covered in twinkling fairy lights. Farooq explained it was the shrine of a holy man.

We enjoyed the breeze for a little longer. I observed a series of manholes but their covers were absent. They were large enough for someone to do themselves an injury, if they were unfortunate enough to fall down one of them. They were systematically placed at intervals along the pavement bordering the beach.

By the wayside, now in the twilight, on the way to the shrine we passed an inert, hunched figure, covered totally in a blanket apart from his toes. Further on we came to numerous busy stalls selling garlands.

Strange men, their torsos draped in chains and numerous beggars surrounded us as Farooq and I took our shoes off, washed our feet and put straw skull caps on. Faisal had disappeared.

At the top of the steps on a balcony covered by an awning were six mounds of garlands. Underneath each, a draped corpse. In the main shrine, men were in deep prayer. A little wooden handrail plated in embossed silver surrounded the tomb itself. Fragments of silver were missing, taken as souvenirs or relics.

Faisal reappeared when we returned the skull caps. The *faqirs*, some only in loin cloths, appeared agitated on our return.

We passed the same hunched figure in the blanket, who hadn't appeared to have moved. Something about his presence filled me with both horror, and awe. Farooq had to wake, or arouse him, to give him a rupee from me.

We found ourselves back at where we had arrived, on a large car and lorry park. It was crowded with swarms of people all wanting buses, rickshaws or taxis. It was only after Faisal had chased many, and with the greatest difficulty we, at last, managed to find a rather slow rickshaw.

24

Flying Back Home with Farooq

At the airport we were a little late and it wasn't possible to get on the flight I had intended, but both Farooq and I managed to confirm seats for the evening one. We returned to the flat, and Farooq went out for fresh milk. He then made Pakistani tea. That is, milk, sugar and tea all boiled together, on this occasion made in an aluminium pot. Wednesday, classed as one of the meatless days, Tuesday being the other, meant red meat was unavailable. The meatless days originated because of shortage, also to give dignity to the poor who can't afford meat. We therefore feasted on white, delicious spiced fried chicken.

Farooq departed to see relatives and a Mr Fayyaz, one of the tenants of the flat, kept me company. He had been a trade union official and told me that steel workers did not earn a living wage, but if someone speaks up for them, he may lose his job, or even disappear.

We returned to the airport at 6.00 pm. Unfortunately, our seats were not confirmed. There were so many pilgrims returning from Mecca and jostling for seats, our reservations were in no way sound. Tomorrow being Christmas day and Quaid-i-Azam's birthday, further compounded the situation. Many people were disappointed, but as it turned out, we were among the fortunate ones.

It was the first time Farooq and I had flown together. I sat in the window seat and told Farooq about a Bengali poem, about travelling light on an aeroplane and renouncing errors and wealth before boarding to go to Vishnu's sphere.

At Lahore airport Choudri, not the man from the village, but another friend of Farooqs' was there to meet us. The people returning from the Haj pilgrimage were having garlands of blossom and strings of rupee notes strung around their necks from relatives and friends. Or were being warmly and lovingly embraced on their return from Mecca.

Choudri said he would not have recognised me. Seemingly we had met on one of my previous visits. We pushed ourselves into his car, in amongst other passengers, and headed for Chamberlain Road. Numerous unlit bicycles wound round the cars on the main road from the airport. We then turned into more obscure lanes.

The good smell of Lahore permeated through the car windows. Buffaloes ambling, tongas pulled by tired horses, rickshaws, scooters and taxis wound through the streets where kebabs were being cooked. Vendors of all commodities sat in dimly lit shops, and there was a hum from the street where crowds were thronging.

Which of the sisters I loved most, Lily, Rehana or Lubna I really didn't know. Memories from previous visits flooded back and so with the feeling of being at home I felt happy to be back and took Anse in my arms, now seven years old. Bilal looked on, still an upright boy, both physically and morally, although at that stage he had given up the task of learning the Quran by heart. Ghazali was asleep in his father's elder brother's, room. Samina and Ghazala resembled Bilal, and were both very beautiful.

We sat in the first reception room, joking and smiling. Ghazala brought tea. I apologised for my delay and unpacked presents such as six lipsticks, nail varnish, French toilet water, cardigans, dinky toys and a steam iron. My father had sent a box of chocolates, I said,

'Not to be opened until Christmas day, I will keep an eye on them through the night!' Anse chose a yellow saloon toy car.

'What about me, what about me.' Lily said in fun, when I gave anything out. It was after midnight when we retired. Lily, Anse and I slept in two beds placed together.

25

Christmas Day, Mohammad Ali Jinnah's Birthday

Everyone was up before me. Ghazali distributed the cars among his brothers and kept changing his mind. Farooq entered the living room and said as it was Christmas he must find a duck. The household was very busy, Ghazala squatting in the kitchen making *chappatis*, Lily and Rehana tidying and attending to the children, Lubna hovering and eyeing me carefully, elder brother heading for the bathroom before prayer.

I gave Bilal some money to buy nuts and Ghazali bought some oranges which Lily said were no good. Bilal returned with a variety of exotic nuts I'd never seen previously, also large raisins and figs. Rehana arranged them all in hand-carved wooden bowls. Farooq interrupted his search for the duck, by returning to mention we were all to go to a wedding party in the evening.

The day wore on and the duck had not arrived. Bilal wanted me to prepare potatoes like I had done last time. I couldn't remember, except I thought I must have creamed them. The potatoes available were all new ones so I just intended to boil them.

At last Farooq arrived with a massive goose. It had just been killed and its feathers were splattered with blood. Lily remarked,

'What a lovely duck.' I laughed and said,

'This is no duck its a fine goose!' Bilal and I both seated on low stools, started the plucking. I would have thought newspapers on the floor to catch the feathers would have been a good idea. But I did not suggest this, knowing the taboo in the house of newspapers on the floor. This was in case there happened to be any reference to God in them.

The mound of feathers grew and we had only finished the front. The wings were very tricky, I needed a break, so Lily took over. The smell of fresh blood on my hands was nauseating and even after washing I couldn't get rid of it. Lily had finished the neck and back, when I returned. The warmth of the bird made me feel even more nauseated. I then cut off its feet and head. Ghazala and Bilal collected the feathers. Further feathers congealed with blood attached themselves to our shoes, but all was washed down and the bird left for Farooq to deal with.

We retreated to the sitting room and eventually Farooq arrived with a massive roasting pot. With a little bit more cleaning and handling of the goose by Farooq, suddenly it took on a very edible beauty. Farooq had worked his culinary magic, yet again. Ghazala had prepared vegetables to accompany the goose in its pot.

The first arrival was Mrs Bashir, who looked ravishing. We had met her husband in Karachi where he had helped to sort out our tickets. She was the first of a steady dribble of people who were gradually filling the apartment. People wafted in from across the yard or up the steps from the street. Many were neighbours and their children.

A party had developed and the doors of the sitting room were closed. Rehana played the *dholak*, a cylindrical drum, with aplomb, there was magic in her fingers. Young girls sang tentatively, Lily's tremulous voice accompanying. Ghazala and some young girls started to dance. When the doors were opened, the smell of cooking goose wafted in, and then everyone left as quietly as they had arrived.

The whole family including elder brother encircled Farooq, as he judiciously carved the bird. Every morsel was devoured, the children licked and sucked each bone clean.

26

The Wedding Party

Lily was buzzing around like a blue bottle, for hours she and Ghazala had been ironing. Our costumes were now laid out on the beds. An orange silk sari with a silver stitched border, and matching blouse, had been prepared for me. Rehana in black attire, showed off her extravagant gold earrings and necklace, she looked dazzling. She helped me to dress and had also arranged silver jewellery to match my sari.

Farooq acted as the perfect chauffeur in Mr Choudri's car. We arrived now in the dark, at a house covered in fairy lights. We, the women, were ushered to a small back room. Around the bare walls was a row of wooden seats. The house had been lent for the wedding party by a brother-in-law of the groom, and this was merely the first part of the marriage celebration.

There were times, especially on this stay, that I felt very alone without Farooq, and this was one of them. In this, women-only room, we made polite conversation. Someone came and placed a chair in our midst. This was for the groom, Naeem. When he came in his face was hardly visible above the garlands and garlands of notes strung around his neck. The women started pushing even more notes into pockets and socks, just about everywhere possible.

We each shook his hand, and wished him well and a young man with a camera snapped pictures at every conceivable opportune moment. Someone assessed just how much money covered Naeem, and the amount was whispered with awe around the members of the room.

After he left, we gradually became aware of the wonderful aromas coming from the kitchen opposite. There was much banging and rattling of plates and pans and people going to and fro. It was obvious the men were being fed first.

Some time later, we too ate out in the garden. I enjoyed the saffron sweet rice with thin sheets of edible silver as decoration. Farooq had told me about the special rice at weddings which was of particular good quality and had been grown using water from wells.

I looked around at the guests, the only men left looked satiated. Farooq was nowhere to be seen. We returned to our room. A boy who kept popping his head around the door was asked by Rehana to find Farooq. He returned to say that Farooq had left, but he did bring some beetle nuts for Rehana and was asked to find cigarettes.

When they came, Lily lit one at a time, and each was passed along the line of women. Older women in Pakistan often are very partial to tobacco, they manage to escape etiquette just like the old lady I had met in the village in 1968.

Rehana, cheered by the beetle nuts, settled herself on the floor with a dholak and one of the younger company started tapping the beat with a spoon. After a few of their songs they insisted I sing. I obliged, and was asked for encores and felt exceedingly flattered, finishing with 'I'm Alabama Bound'! The older women said although they did not understand the words they knew the meaning. The evening whizzed by.

27

Chilly Undertones and a Warm Breeze

The next morning I found myself outside in the yard, at the back of the apartment, listening to the children read. English was learnt at school from a very early age. Farooq interrupted Bilal with what seemed to be rather fatuous comments.

I thought I should take advantage of Farooq's presence so sat next to him. We strangely talked of the weather, then I asked why he was avoiding me. We had been writing quite warmly before the visit.

No doubt I had not been easy on him and he was preoccupied with his film and part of the problem was money, or lack of it. As far as I was concerned I achieved nothing by our conversation, and felt disappointed afterwards.

This must have been apparent because Lily and Rehana kept asking what was wrong. Eventually I gave in and told them. They said I should talk to Aftab. He would be coming on Monday.

That evening the Rafiques called. I hadn't seen them since their visit to Cumbria in 1971. They suggested I stay with them over the following weekend when Farooq would be in Karachi attending the second part of the wedding.

That night I had difficulty sleeping and was glad when morning came. I found Anse's presence a great comfort, he seemingly had adopted me. Thoughts had been reawakened with a resonance; they being of meeting Doctor Aftab again.

Of the time we first met in 1968 and the way he had looked at the small gifts I had brought from England, the visits to Nankana, the gifts he gave me....

At the Rafiques, I met Mrs Rafique's sister and her husband, who was Press Secretary to the Governor of the Punjab. He showed me his office, situated in lavish gardens. He also bestowed upon me numerous books on Pakistan stamped with the compliments of Mohammed Amanullah Khan. Behind all this, a soft medley played at the back of my mind, thinking of seeing Aftab again.

Back in the home, Bilal had gone to Nankana and although Anse was around, I missed his older brother. On the Monday we did not wait around for the Doctor, and Lily and Rehana accompanied me to Anarkali for presents for me to take back. These were a wooden hand carved box for my father, a stuffed mongoose for my mother, a brass plate for my aunt Eleanor, and ornamental slippers for my sisters. We also visited again the wonderful *chaat* parlours.

Although Aftab did not arrive that day, I was not alarmed, I knew he would come when he could. He arrived late in the morning of the following day. I don't know where I had been, but he was sitting in the sitting room when I walked through the door. He rose from his seat and shook my hand, immaculately dressed in a buff suit, white shirt and maroon tie. He looked so much younger than I remembered and I couldn't conceal my pleasure in seeing him.

He asked about my family and I told him my parents were separated. He said that he was sorry and looked down at his hands. He spoke proudly about his now three children.

The conversation veered, I don't know how toward President Bhutto and his parents, especially his mother. His voice became soft as he explained how Bhutto had taken power. Perhaps all this was matter of fact but it appeared like a stream of poetic thoughts when he spoke. He asked if I wanted to talk to him about something. I think any reason for the meeting had dissolved. I don't know why I said it but I said I thought he wanted to talk to me.

He kept looking at his watch. He said he needed to have his passport photograph taken and return to Nankana. His eyes seemed full as were mine.

Later, when he returned he invited Lily and I to Nankana—he wished to talk about Farooq to me. We were to catch the 1.00 pm train the following day.

28

Nankana Again

Rehana, Lily and I headed for the bazaar once more prior to the visit to Nankana. I wished to buy some silver filigree jewellery and needed to compare quality and prices. This was for samples to perhaps sell back home. I found the prices had trebled since my last visit in '73. When at last I decided on a particular trader we left the shop thinking the train could still be caught, but without me asking for a receipt. It wasn't until we were seated in the tonga that I realised. Lily and I left Rehana, and sped back to the shop, although by that time we knew we had missed the train.

It was on that outing I had followed two women down a street thinking they were Lily and Rehana. I couldn't understand why another woman was pulling at my sleeve. The other woman was Lily! I had followed two complete strangers in *burqas* down a whole street!

We did catch the 6.00 p.m. train and Anse accompanied us. He gripped my hand with excitement at the station. The height of the train was about four feet from the platform. We scrambled up, Bilal, who had just returned from Nankana had come to see us off. The train started to pull out of the station before Bilal jumped off. Above us was a sign which said seven people only to a seat. On all the seats there were nine or ten. A gush of wind entered through a gap, where there was once a door, it was all very bracing. We left the dull lights of Lahore through the suburbs, Shahdara Bagh Junction, and into the country. Anse's face was pressed to the window, not wishing to miss anything, Lily and I chuckled at him.

At the stations vendors entered the compartment displaying piles of hot delicacies on plates. At Sheikhupura Junction Lily had struck up a conversation with a young lady; she too happened to be called Rehana, and wished to talk to me. Lily and I swapped places.

The lady introduced me to her family and said she liked reading Georgette Heyer. She spoke quietly and very sweetly. I asked to see her face, as I found it difficult to speak to someone whose face I couldn't see. She told me her father-in-law was very strict, but raised her veil for an instant. She was indeed very beautiful, I thought it rather sad that she was obliged to conceal this beauty.

She told me about her brother-in-law who had been let down by his prospective wife in Sweden where he was a chemical engineer. He had returned here to find a wife and they were on their way to a party to which, after speaking to him, I was invited. I thanked them, but declined.

Now looking back at our stay at Nankana I don't recall any conversation with the Doctor about Farooq. I do remember him playing the *tabla* and his singing. In translation the verses meant the real love in life will be united in death. It seemed again like slow motion when he took my hand in the street to say farewell, probably all too sadly, a final time.

Part Four

Part Four

29

England and Pakistan

Farooq married a very fine looking lady. I had met her in Pakistan at the marriage celebration in 1976, and later they were to have one daughter. I married too, a Scotsman and we had a son and a daughter. My marriage did not last, so I brought the children up mainly on my own. Lily and Rehana visited me a number of times and stayed during the eighties. After that, we didn't write frequently. But Bilal did contact me prior to coming to England to study. He required information about University courses. When he came here, he started to visit at regular intervals. Later Ghazali was to join him in England, both to study, then to work, as did Bilal.

My children are now in their twenties, but we all had a bit of a shock when I was diagnosed with cancer in 2002. Nothing really could be taken for granted anymore. Like many sufferers it can make you concentrate in life on what you think to be important. Therefore, when Bilal suggested I visit Pakistan again in November 2003, I grabbed at the opportunity.

After years in Cumbria hardly travelling abroad, except to France in the seventies, and talk of terrorism after 9/11, it was with trepidation I journeyed by train to Manchester Airport. The sun filtered through a grey haze, warming the morning. A Virgin train spokeswoman warned over the Tannoy that if the person who had been smoking in the toilet, which was disgusting, was caught, they would be put off the train at the next stop!

Armed police stood around due to a perceived terrorist threat, whilst we queued at Manchester Airport—it all felt rather threatening. I was a little shocked that this was now Britain. Thankfully, it was not long before we headed for Baku 33,000 feet in the air at 571 mph.

Over Afghanistan, a young Sikh introduced himself to me. He was a musician and travelling to make a video in Lahore. He also happened to be doing some Indian music workshops in Cumbria in the New Year. Mangeet and I swapped telephone numbers. An hour, 500 miles to our destination, Lahore, I put my watch to Pakistani time, 6.00 am and wrote:

A ribbon of carmen, yellow stretches across the sky.
Marking where the grey blue matter of cloud
ends, and limitless egg shell blue begins,
and this is the welcome over Pakistan
on now, the 15th November 2003.

We settled like a bird on Pakistani soil and eventually I found my suitcase, after I had given up all hope. Not quite at the exit it smelt as if there was a fire nearby. Outside there was a hill of people, some had large placards with the name of the person they were looking for. At the front of the mound of people but about a third of the way up the road I saw a little round face; although about 30 metres away I recognised Lily! I gave a nervous wave not absolutely sure I could recognise her so far away. She flung her arm in the air, it was her. We embraced and Ahmed, Bilal's brother had brought his car to collect me.

I asked Lily if there had been a fire? She appeared puzzled. Obviously not aware of the smell. I later learnt it was due to traffic pollution, the rickshaws were especially blamed. I read that the government tried to enforce the owners to put silencers, to reduce fumes, on the offending vehicles, but the owners were reluctant because they said silencers restricted the mileage they could achieve.

It did not take long to appreciate that Lahore had grown enormously in my absence. The popular estimate of population now being at nine million. Although I did not see nomadic settlements, the poverty seemed much more insidious and more broadly spread. In the seventies there were about 14 rupees to the pound, now there were roughly 100.

The family had moved from their old apartment to one of the new residential areas at Cavalry Ground. Bilal and Ghazali had largely financed the building of their new home. It was spacious and easily kept clean with six bedrooms en suite.

Soon into my stay, it did occur to me all over again that with all the British influence, due to the Raj, a Pakistani going to Britain would not find life so foreign. It is something that we too often forget back home. Pakistani customs may appear foreign to us but the same is not true vice versa. Many of us in England have either forgotten about the Raj or don't know about it.

We have so many common words; pen, light bulb, train, sofa, glass, cup, underwear and many, many more. Some origins of food dishes appear unclear. For example, did the trifle originate from India or did the British influence dishes of the Indians, or both?

A love of tea drinking is shared by both. Then there are all the systems the British left, the civil service, the bureaucracy running the rail network and the post office. Also, I found the Pakistani's share a love of chrysanthemums. The Horticultural Society of Pakistan having an annual show at Race Course Park. Then there are Colleges, the High Court, Police Station, Punjab University, Criminal Investigation Agency Building and the Assembly Rooms all built during the Raj. The style could be called British with a Mughal flavour. Sports which they love most in Pakistan are cricket, polo and hockey. Furthermore, the founder of Pakistan, Mohammed Ali Jinnah from all accounts and from photographs had modelled himself on the perfect English gentleman.

Something else which made me think, was some restoration work in Lahore Fort. The Sikhs and British damaged some carved marble panels when fighting. Although the restoration work done by the British was not quite up to the standard of the original, the fact that this was done at all, I thought, was remarkable. I could not see this respect of heritage extending to American damage in Iraq and Afghanistan

In the home I could not help remarking about the picture of Buckingham Palace in the dining room. Rehana told me in was a tea towel I had brought in 1968 which they liked, and had framed. In the living room there was a print of the Haywain!

30

Iftari and Visits

I hadn't appreciated the stress caused by not eating or drinking during daylight. Lily had tried to delay my visit, due I think to this. I have to say this stress wasn't apparent, there were no harsh words but I could see it took great concentration and the prayers helped. Everyone cheered up when *Iftari* was being prepared, the breaking of the fast at 5.00 p.m., just when the sun was setting. I read in the *Dawn* newspaper about how people sometimes had accidents hurriedly driving home for Iftari.

At this tea we usually had the now famous fruit *chaat*, spicy battered potatoes and dates. Straight after the meal there were prayers on the television. During the night, about 3.00 a.m. someone passed beating a drum, very loudly. It was quite frightening and intimidating at first. This was to waken people for prayer and eating. Often too, during the night you would hear whistles being blown, close by and further afield. Most of the streets, in the district, had armed guards, who stood in little sentry boxes. I think they used whistles as a sort of alarm.

After Iftari we usually had an evening meal just before bed. It was as if the clock for eating was just transposed to night-time. I admired the fact no one ate or drank anything during daylight. A month of this was some achievement. I had arrived in the middle of Ramadan. People told me it was not so difficult at this time of year. Ramadan depending on cycles of the moon could fall at any time of year. The long hot days of summer were a much greater challenge.

There is no good time to say that there were two very sad changes in the intervening years of my absence. They being the sad death of dear Lubna, she had died before they moved to their new home. The other was the death of elder brother. Both deaths were a great loss to all the family.

The first two weeks of my stay being part of Ramadan, to give some relief to the family I took advantage of Javaid's expertise. He had become an established guide showing diplomats around Lahore. Unfortunately, since 9/11 there were not many visitors to guide. I felt quite honoured visiting Lahore Fort, Jehangir's Mausoleum, Shalimar Gardens, Lahore Museum accompanied by his excellent knowledge.

He usually commandeered a rickshaw which he brought around to the house to pick me up. We would roar with the loud two stroke engine, ejecting fumes across Lahore. The logic, if any, of the traffic again totally eluding me. Vehicles did not even slow down, never mind stop, when entering a major road. As far as I could see halt signs were non existent. Bikes, cars or rickshaws looped out miraculously from small side turnings into the main thoroughfare of traffic. Somewhere in the distant past I recall Farooq having told me that this was in order not to interrupt the flow!

Whereever we went it was obvious I was walking in the shadow of Rory Stewart, whom Javaid had met some years previously. At the rather plundered tomb of Shah Jehan's wet nurse, I was told Rory Stewart had spent hours doing the most intricate drawings. Perhaps Javaid was disappointed that my interest was not as intense as his had been. He insisted I contact Rory on my return. Recently in an attempt, I spoke to his mother who said Rory's book, *The Places In Between* about walking through Afghanistan, post American invasion, will come out in the summer.

I asked Javaid to take me to the main post office. Not only is sending a letter reliable in Pakistan but they have recently restored the main post office. I could not resist taking photographs, what a pleasant place, with balconies and a central courtyard! The wooden counters have now been replaced with ones of solid marble. At a time when we are closing our post offices, this would be an edifice almost to die for!

On one of our return journeys we had a rickshaw driver with a finely tuned motor giving it extra speed. He was obviously very proud of his vehicle and his confidence was such that he didn't give way to anything, including buses! At one point our road was jammed with traffic. Our unconcerned driver did not stop, he just took to the other side of the road, and took on all the oncoming traffic. His bravado was hair raising, Javaid saved the situation by telling the driver we needed to look out for a left turning and we eventually returned to the correct side of the road.

The stories in the paper were indeed gruesome of the most horrendous accidents. Head on collisions with buses, metal pipes or rods slipping off carts or lorries, people being decapitated, were some. Danger from terrorism was negligible compared to the likelihood of a road accident.

Apart from the American, Daniel Pearl I was not aware of anyone else being kidnapped and executed.

Returning from Jehangir's Mausoleum, Javaid took me to see Doctor Aftab. It was in a rather poor district. There was much dust and debris. The Doctor met me at his door. He said he did not know what to expect as Javaid had told him I had put weight on. I was surprised that he had read one of the earlier drafts of this book and had wanted to write to me every day ever since. The dampener on this was that he had not had time. During the day he looked after his beautiful granddaughter, and from late afternoon had a long surgery.

It did not take much time for me to realise that I still felt the same way about him. It seemed unbelievable after so much time, and each having lived such different lives, had not destroyed the feeling. About a year after my previous visit Aftab had gone to work in Iran. He was there for seventeen years and saw little of his wife.

In Iran he was in a horrendous car accident. His driver had failed to see a large stone at the side of the road. This had resulted in plates in his legs and one leg shorter than the other.

Yet I could not help remarking just how fit he looked, and how young! Then there was the heart bypass operation which had not been the success that was hoped for. He had apparently left the operation for too long, so that the damage was too great.

He had been in Iran when the Kurds had been gassed. This was not far from where he lived. He said they looked as if they had just gone to sleep. He was referring to nerve gas, which had been used on them by the Iraqis. Before we left he said he would visit me at the weekend.

31

Eid, Aftab and Artists

I could not wait until the weekend but then, it was thought inappropriate by Rehana that Aftab should visit me. In a country where the only support financial and emotional is found in families, it is vital for its members to respect one another, almost a matter of life or death in some circumstances.

If anyone made me happy in my life, it was Aftab. I met him again during the Eid celebration, the feasting after Ramadan. Everyone said *Eid Mubarak* to each other, wishes of good wishes.

Lily had taken me up to the yard at the top of the house to show me the Eid moon with a solitary star. It was so sharp in the early night sky, I was in awe of the beauty.

Even in Pakistan Eid is celebrated on different nights as there is always controversy about the correct night depending on the moon cycle. There was talk in the newspapers about standardising it, so that the Eid celebration would be the same throughout the country. Variations between countries are even more marked depending on their position on the globe.

There was no doubt in my mind staring at this moon and this star that it had to be the correct night here. I asked Lily if it was the same moon and star on her national flag. She said she didn't know.

Aftab told me that night about two things he thought to be most important. The first, the two and a half per cent of savings given to the poor by all Muslims on a yearly basis called *zakat*. This is distinct from gifts given after Ramadan called *Eidie*, and from other charitable distributions that are not mandatory in Islam but recommended. The second was not to talk about intimate relationships, not to betray others. I hope he doesn't feel I am betraying him by writing, or that I ever would betray him. The time I was with him made me feel I was still alive.

Javaid continued to escort me on the tourist trail. We visited Shakir Ali's house. The artist had worked with the leading architects of the day designing his house and it had taken ten years to build. Ancient dark thick wooden doors were perfectly inaugurated into the building and contrasted beautifully with the intricate modern brick work. All the windows and doors were arched and elongated, some so much so, that at one end of the studio they looked church-like, and reminded me of Chagall's work.

In the garden was a raised dais, its top covered in grass. There were seats made out of slabs of stone around the edge of the area. The purpose being to seat an audience at musical evenings, the dais being for the musicians. At the far end of the small garden was a small kitchen to feed the audience and entertainers. Sadly, Shakir Ali died just after the house was completed. He did not have the pleasure of living there.

We also visited the Chughtai Museum, named after Pakistan's leading modern painter, who died in 1975. The museum is run by the artist's son, Abdur Rahman Chughtai who has recently commissioned and designed an octagonal building as the first phase of expanding the museum. There is a fountain in the middle of the interior, from which eight channels take the water out through holes to the outside of the building, where it trickles down each facet.

Mr Chughtai was very accommodating and took us around the pictures himself. The artwork displayed how Chughtai senior had worked, from very intricate fine pencil drawings. Although the work was detailed it also incorporated large areas of flat colour. Most of all, I loved the poetic content.

Chughtai junior mentioned that Buckingham Palace had been in touch with him regarding a missing Chughtai, a portrait of the Queen, from Windsor Castle. They had needed a description of the picture. He thought perhaps the Princes had something to do with it. I said perhaps it was Princess Diana in order to give it to her Pakistani boyfriend. Chughtai praised the latter, saying Hasnat Khan was the only one who had not spoken intimately about her.

Javaid had mentioned Princess Diana when we passed King Edward College where both Aftab and Hasnat had trained to be doctors. The Princess had visited the College. She was also said to have visited Hasnat's mother. Sadly, the mother had not agreed to the relationship because it was thought that because of Diana's status there would be no peace for their family.

The painter Chughtai seemingly had lived close to Javaid's old house in Chamberlain Road. Later, from photographs, both Javaid and Lily remembered seeing him. I think he must have stood out, for he seemed extremely individualistic.

I think my enthusiasm about his work impressed his son. He gave me prints, a book and posters, I was quite overwhelmed. When I returned I posted a card of thanks and he has recently written and told me I was the visitor of the year, and he would be in touch.

Still in Lahore, Javaid and I visited the very much alive and renowned watercolourist, Dr Ajaz Anwar at the National College of Art. He is a friend of Javaid's and they both share a great love of old Lahore.

Dr Ajaz had some folding spectacles in a dinky case, they looked very expensive, but he said he had bought them for a pittance on a stall in the Mall. They were Chinese. I had heard Chinese vegetables were also under-cutting prices and flooding the market. When Javaid and I were at Jehangir's tomb we met a group of wealthy looking Far Easterners we thought would be Japanese. We were very surprised that they turned out to be Chinese!

When Dr Ajaz heard about this book he mentioned his friend, Dr Ian Talbot, whom I have now contacted and I am just hoping that he may like what I have written. It is not just a long shot—it is the only shot!

I made one outing with Zulfiqar who took me around Lawrence Gardens. From a large Banyan tree with great buttresses came the strangest sounds, and on looking up I saw a mass of large bats and couldn't resist taking a photo. Also in the same park we saw the memorial garden of Fatima Jinnah, Mohammed Ali Jinnah's supportive sister, and known as the Mother of Pakistan. Neither Javaid nor Zulfiqar are married and although I admire both, it is unfortunate I have feelings for the brother who is.

Just before I left, Aftab rang me saying he wanted my father to wait for him three or four years. What did he mean? Dare I continue to dream? My head still has a tendency to swim when I think of him.

When I left Lahore again, the warmth extended to me, and the respect and care showered on me by the immediate and the extended family made me feel a more complete person. *Inshallah*, it will go on.

Bilal has just rung to say he is leaving for Pakistan today in order to make arrangements for his wedding. I told him that I wished I was going with him. Lily, I hope, will visit me in the summer, that is, if arrangements can be made for her to enter the country. I will fill in her sponsorship form, so it does, and will ... go on.